Praise For
BUILDING STRONG HUMAN BRIDGES: *TEN TOOLS FOR SUCCESS*

We've all met them. We've had them enter our lives, either personally or professionally. You know when they are in your midst. They are a very special kind of leader—calm, humble, quietly confident, thoughtful, caring and undeniably capable—they are the natural "teachers."

In every difficult situation, leaders ask themselves, "Do I have the tools I need to lead in this situation?" In his new book, *Building Strong Human Bridges: Ten Tools for Success*, author Harry Amend not only pulls back the curtain to share in detail those "essential tools" he has used to be so successful professionally, he also shares keen examples of situations where each of those tools were effectively used. The following chapters will provide a ring-side seat as you watch a true "Master Teacher and Coach" at work.

–Dr. Rich McBride, retired Educational Service District Superintendent

In a world where we're all growing further and further apart, *Building Strong Human Bridges: Ten Tools for Success* is a GOLD MINE! As a mentor to many, Harry has lived and breathed these ten proven strategies for laying a foundation for healthy, thriving relationships in every area of our lives. For me, learning these ten tools has helped change the dynamic and trajectory of my most important relationships, including my work life and, at my own kitchen table. The Action Plans at the end of each chapter also helped me to put these ten tools into effect in my therapy practice, as I work with my clients to improve connections in every area of their lives. For anyone looking to connect, or reconnect, look no further than this book.

–Chris Haas M.A. M.F.T.I., CEO of Maui Marriage and Family Therapy

Reading *Building Strong Human Bridges: Ten Tools for Success* is like applying a balm to the roughest of leadership challenges. Harry Amend's ability to weave common sense and common, caring approaches, along with his natural storytelling ability make this book practical, applicable, and entertaining to read. His Ten Tools remind us that conflict does not have to be a deal breaker to success, rather by applying these strategies, teams can be made stronger through mutual respect, trust and knowing they are heard. This book is not just ideal for the new or seasoned leader, but a valuable resource for building strong and healthy bridges at home with our families and friends.

–Stacy A Barney, Assistant Center Director The Salvation Army Kroc Center

I was honored to work with Harry Amend during his tenure as a Middle School Principal. He has captured real life examples, practical techniques, and effective connection strategies that build upon his philosophy of life. He shares with the reader actionable techniques to increase trust, build relationships and promote a positive and effective long-term team culture. *Building Strong Human Bridges: Ten Tools for Success* is a roadmap for administrators, teachers, and any leader to improve relationships in every environment, especially the challenging ones. In my career, I often relied upon Harry's thoughtful guidance and the tools explored in this book. It never failed me.

–Glenna Bouge, Retired Administrator, Academic Coach

I've known "Coach Amend" for 50 years, and he's helped me in many facets of my life. He's mentored me in leadership, conflict resolution, marital advice, spiritual leadership, and child rearing challenges. As a 1st line manager with a Fortune 100 company over the past 22 years, I have had Coach present the Ten Tools to my leadership teams in two different states. His book, *Building Strong Human Bridges: Ten Tools for Success*, is a guide book for anyone who wants to improve their ability to build and maintain strong trust bridges in every area of their life. Each chapter provides strategies and stories that are guideposts to human bridge building.

–Jim Lusk, CFP, CLV, ChFC, MEd

BUILDING STRONG
HUMAN BRIDGES

TEN TOOLS FOR SUCCESS

HARRY AMEND

Building Strong Human Bridges
Ten Tools for Success

© 2021, Harry Amend.

Print ISBN: 978-1-09838-979-6 | eBook ISBN: 978-1-09838-980-2

CONTENTS

BIOGRAPHY

A 41-year veteran in education, Harry Amend spent 32 years of his career as a teacher, coach, counselor, principal and superintendent in the Spokane Valley, Washington area. As President of the 1,500-member Washington Association of School Administrators (WASA) in the late 1990's, Harry joined Superintendent of Public Instruction, Teri Bergeson, and Governor, Gary Locke, in leading education reform in Washington.

As Superintendent of school districts in northwest Montana and North Idaho for a total of nine years, Harry was a leader in both states in efforts to implement school reform. Harry always brought a strong emphasis toward at-risk and special needs students to his leadership positions. He brought the middle school "School within a School" model and the first Bridge Academy dropout retrieval high schools to both Montana and Idaho.

Harry was a finalist for Superintendent of the Year in Washington in 1998 and in Idaho in 2007. One of Harry's favorite part-time jobs was serving as a major league baseball scout for the Philadelphia Phillies for twenty years. Harry currently lives in Twin Lakes Village in North Idaho with his wife Sandy. Their three grown children and spouses, Gregg (Shandra) Jake, Abbie, Molly, Luke, Mike (Megan) Easton, and Karie (Ben) Isaac, Nate, Jenna, and Tyler, live less than an hour away in the Spokane area.

Contact: Harry Amend, 21917 N. Molly Lane, Rathdrum, ID 83858, Cell: 208-929-0344, Email: h.amend@haploos.com

DEDICATION

This book is dedicated to Sandy, my amazing wife of more than 51-years and the most patient and caring person on the planet. It's also dedicated to my brother Dex whose unconditional love and patience got me off to a good start in life. Finally, this book is dedicated to Luke, our very special grandson who has taught our family new definitions of love and of life.

ACKNOWLEDGEMENTS

I'd like to thank every educator who puts their key in the ignition, backs their car out of the driveway, and answers the bell every day to serve our students. Why do these dedicated people show up every day? It is because they know they have the most important job in our society—building people. They are master bridge-builders, connecting with kids and bringing hope. Every day, they are motivating, guiding, and persisting. In addition to academics, these heroes teach the values and the tools necessary for success and happiness. They are building our next generation and helping each student to believe in themselves and in their ability to have a good life.

I wrote this book from March 2020 - February of 2021 when the world was quarantined because of the Coronavirus pandemic. It was the year when countless parents around the world sat at their kitchen tables and tried to manage and teach their own children. Reading, writing, fractions, quadratic equations, photosynthesis, current world events, politics, —YIKES!! One of the positive takeaways from this pandemic tragedy will be a worldwide boost in the admiration, love, and support for teachers. I hope one outcome of the pandemic is that adults in every community on earth continue to hold a higher level of respect for the crucial role educators play in the lives of children, and in the future of our planet.

Building Strong Human Bridges: Ten Tools for Success is a timely tribute to a world that has been disconnected by COVID-19. Unspeakable images of human separation and dying have been indelibly seared into our minds. At the same time, our hearts have been blessed by inspiring images of true heroism and uncommon human compassion. May the rebuilding of the human bridges that will reconnect our world begin with you.

A special acknowledgement goes out to my Canadian team, three retired educators and a young tech guy, Tom, who bailed us out every day. To Jimmy, Schwenk, and Webby, three world-class people who joined me in a great adventure into the unknown. For three years, we traveled into the hinterlands of Alberta, Canada teaching the *Ten Tools for Success* and other leadership skills to executives, mid-managers, and individual contributors working on the well-heads. These three guys could take a punch and handle a tough crowd. Sometimes they shared tears, and sometimes they were stand-up comics. With every personality, life story, and family situation, we saw people grow in their bridge-building skills. A very diverse group at the beginning, we saw these rugged, strong-willed individuals become a caring and highly effective team.

To my editor for this book, Shelly Shaffer, a woman of incredible insights and skill.

And finally, a special thank you to Dr. Randy Russell, my longtime friend and colleague who encouraged me to write *Building Strong Human Bridges: Ten Tools for Success* and was a great help throughout the writing process.

AUTHOR'S NOTE

The first time I saw physical violence, I was seven years old. It was 1952, and I was at a community playground in Charlotte, North Carolina when I watched a group of White kids beat up a Black kid about their age. The first seeds for this book were planted in my young heart that day. My sadness and sense of helplessness from witnessing such violence turned into a lifelong effort to support underdogs of all ages, shapes, and sizes.

My career in serving people taught me that communication is the key to healing. Connecting with a nod, a hug, or just the right words brings hope to the toughest of situations. *Building Strong Human Bridges: Ten Tools for Success* began after a slammed door in my office as a first-year high school counselor in 1976. After a deadlocked conversation with a family in crisis, I sputtered to myself, "Why won't they just focus on solving this and quit worrying about winning it?" This became "Solve it—Don't Win It (SIDWI)," the first of *The Ten Tools for Success.*

Over my twelve years as a counselor, nine additional tools joined the list. As I moved into other leadership roles, I taught *The Ten Tools for Success* to every team I led. I wanted my teams to experience the positive impact of the strong, bridge-building communication tools I had learned firsthand. Each team learned to focus on choosing just the right words for the conversation at hand, and the importance of preparation and practice, especially for the toughest conversations.

My motivation for finally writing *Building Strong Human Bridges: Ten Tools for Success* was to share this set of tools with any person who is open to enhancing their own ability to better connect with people in a positive way. The stories in the book are intended to clarify, encourage, and provide insight, and possibly a chuckle. I hope they will support you in every area of your life.

I chose to write *Building Strong Human Bridges: Ten Tools for Success* at this time for two reasons. First, people over the years have shared stories of how the practical nature of *the ten tools* had a positive impact on their lives, both professionally and personally. Their encouragement was a key factor in writing the book. Second, I started writing the book while I was quarantined with my wife during the COVID-19 pandemic in the spring of 2020. The worldwide health issues, merging with economic and social unrest, challenged the world, and shone a light on the need for quality communication and building strong human bridges during these difficult times.

INTRODUCTION

When we hear the phrase "building a bridge," several thoughts may come to mind. We might think about the physical process of building a bridge over a river or railroad track. We might think about creating a bridge for our mouth. We might also think about doing something to help opposing groups of people to understand each other or develop a relationship with someone else.

In author Harry Amend's new book *Building Strong Human Bridges*, the reader is introduced to the *"Ten Tools for Success."* With each tool, Harry shares strategies and stories that are both beneficial and impactful. This book helps at home, at work, and in life.

This book should be required reading for anyone who wants to work with other people successfully. Harry provides valuable insights, experiences, and situations that will connect with readers personally and professionally in a valuable and easy to read format. Harry's time-tested leadership strategies help everyone from the first-time leader to the seasoned veteran, from the kitchen table to the boardroom.

Building Strong Human Bridges: Ten Tools for Success is the story about how to treat people with dignity and respect, lead with our values, and ultimately develop, and bring out the best in ourselves and in those we interact with every day. Harry speaks from experience and provides an insightful and well-written guide. He provides a realistic and practical blueprint to follow in order for each of us to be successful working with others.

Isaac Newton once stated, "We build too many walls and not enough bridges." *Building Strong Human Bridges: Ten Tools for Success* offers the practical tools, along with an inspirational and motivational lift, we need for ourselves, our families, teams, and organizations to be successful.

It is a must read for anyone who aspires to develop stronger relationships, connect more deeply, and build stronger bridges with mutual respect, dignity, and kindness.

–Dr. Randy Russell

BUILDING BRIDGES

I've been building human bridges my entire life. Since 1987, I've used *The Ten Tools for Success* to train educators, bankers, insurance professionals, and dentists. I've trained oilmen running wellheads in isolated locations of Canada, and power company lineman whose dangerous work took them to the top of power poles during blinding blizzards or ice storms. I've supported counselors, therapists, nonprofits, and everyday people who wanted to learn how to strengthen the human bridges in their lives. As with any construction tool, learning the basics comes first, including being ready to take risks to improve. The good news is, even as a beginner, every time one or more of the tools is used, you will grow. These tools create positive connections and build strong human bridges. They enrich, empower, and heal those that use them. As you explore the tools, you'll learn that your success with each of the ten tools can lead to building strong bridges between individuals, and with groups of people.

Physical Bridges

The purpose of any physical bridge is to carry cargo from point A to point B. There are many different types of bridges in the world. A mail courier in the Amazon jungle might use a series of rope bridges to cross when the terrain is too difficult to build a road. Two of the primary east-west bridges in Seattle, Washington are eight lane bridges that float on Lake Washington, carrying thousands of commuters a day. Some military bridges are portable, but still need to support the weight of multiple military tanks. Even popsicle stick bridges created in engineering courses test students' ability to engineer a bridge that will hold a heavy load. Depending on their purpose, each of these bridges is built to meet the special needs of those crossing the bridge.

For decades, engineering students have competed in bridge-building contests. At a recent competition, students built a bridge that supported a weight of over 1,000 pounds. The only building materials allowed were popsicle sticks and Elmer's glue. Along the way, the students learned important lessons. By trial and error, they learned that for the greatest strength, the sticks needed to be patiently glued together one stick at a time. When too much weight was attempted too soon, the bridge collapsed. In repairing the bridge, the students learned that broken sticks, sticks that had been glued back together, ended up being stronger than the new sticks. This lesson can help us when we consider building trust bridges between people; sometimes, a bridge that is repaired becomes stronger than the original bridge.

In life, we sometimes face unexpected adversity that might damage our bridges. We've all probably driven or walked on bridges in windy weather and felt the power of the wind as the bridge swayed. Natural disasters, such as strong winds, can destroy even the strongest bridges. In an epic wind storm in 1940, news footage of the Tacoma Narrows Bridge showed the high steel support towers swaying and the huge suspension cables straining as the bridge was pummeled by the storm. The concrete highway, held together with wrought iron, convulsed wildly and finally dropped into the water below. The bridge was not strong enough to withstand the storm. Every bridge—including both physical and emotional bridges—has load limits, needing a foundation strong enough to carry cargo safely, even in stormy weather.

Bridges of Trust

History's messages are clear, building bridges requires the proper use of materials, tools, teamwork, and tenacity. A strong analogy exists between carefully building a stick bridge and the patience required to build a bridge of trust between humans. Trust is the glue of human bridge-building. Trust bridges must be built slowly. Human trust bridges can grow stronger from the failures and lessons learned during the communication process. Often, the heaviest weight in human bridge-building is the emotion brought to a situation and the ensuing conversation. A key focus in this book is learning specific, tangible tools to process these emotions and build stronger bridges.

As I share in the first chapter, "Solve It—Don't Win It— (SIDWI)" is the step-by-step approach that produces trust, the Elmer's glue, which holds the human bridge together. If two people address an emotional load that is too heavy before a strong enough trust bridge is built, the relationship slips back to ground zero or worse. If that slip happens, SIDWI needs to be restarted to provide fresh glue to mend the break in the bridge. Improvement in a relationship is not like a two-position light switch, with the light (or trust) being on or off. Rather, it is more like turning the dial on a dimmer switch, the light/trust getting brighter little by little. In building trust bridges, we succeed, fail, learn, tweak, apply glue, and then try again. This book focuses on building bridges and building people. You will learn how to support, nurture, and heal, even in the most difficult situations.

The Ten Tools

In each kitchen, garage, or shed, there are tools. Each tool has a specific purpose, shape, and design to assist with the project at hand. Like the tools in the shed, *The Ten Tools for Success* are tangible. These tools are strategies that can improve anyone's personal and professional relationships. Whether it's at the kitchen table, at the operating table, in the conference room, or at a traffic stop, *The Ten Tools* help with communication, relationships, and connections. The right tools, with careful practice, are the keys to personal and professional success.

In this book, each chapter discusses how the reader sharpens their own communication tools. These tools can lead anyone to greatness as a leader, a spouse, or a parent. To support each of the following chapters, I've selected stories to illustrate how the tools can be successful in real-life situations. Some of these stories are sad, some are happy, and some are funny. These examples show how a person's success or failure is driven by the tools they possess and by how well they use those tools.

Activities at the end of each chapter provide a deeper dive into how to start using the tool explored in the chapter. At the conclusion of *Building Strong Human Bridges: Ten Tools for Success*, a template for a personal action plan shares steps to begin incorporating *The Ten Tools* into the reader's personal and professional life.

Navigating a conversation about emotional topics can be the toughest of all leadership challenges. "Tool #1: Solve It—Don't Win It" focuses on how to listen, learn, and then lead. Success in using SIDWI relies heavily on the gatekeeper of all tools—the ability to positively connect with people. In Chapter 1, readers learn specific words and behaviors to build strong bridges of trust. Managing tough, emotional situations is always a heavy load, so these bridges need to be sturdy.

I've been in situations where I've been wronged, and I was mad. My emotions were high, and I knew I needed to get myself under control before I moved into a conversation. "Tool #2: Leave the Sledgehammer in the Pickup" uses the analogy of comparing the many hammers used in construction with the different approaches an effective leader uses to achieve successful conversations. Chapter 2 focuses on ways to preserve dignity, avoid bullying, and care about what is going on in the other person's life. The reader learns how to use the best hammer to get the job done.

"Tool #3: Don't Major in the Minors" focuses on the need to prioritize in order to reduce stress. In Chapter 3, I share three, controllable concepts and strategies to deal with stressors. I have learned that if I stop and react to every negative word or incident I see or hear; I won't have time left to build my team or pursue its goals. Following the tips of "Don't Major in the Minors" helps me manage my time so I can lead my team and still have time for my family and myself.

"Tool #4: The 95% Rule" comes into play when I make a decision that impacts the whole team in order to change the behavior of a small percentage of the team who are not complying. This mistake has broad, negative impacts on a team. Failure to directly confront the negative behavior of the "5%" empowers them. In Chapter 4, I share strategies for successfully navigating this common challenge. The focus is on honoring and supporting positive, hardworking people while learning words and strategies to deal firmly with people that aren't buying in.

"Tool #5: Don't Kick a Sleeping Doberman" is about navigating the emotions of the change process. Examples, including when you should immediately intervene and when you should just monitor and let people process on their own, help to clarify the factors in these important decisions. Because either decision comes with its own set of consequences, in Chapter 5, I offer criteria to help with decision-making (i.e. when to step in or when to step back). The chapter concludes with a discussion of the challenges new leaders face when joining a team.

"Tool #6: You Can't Please Everyone, But You Can Treat Everyone Right" digs deeper into selecting the best words and strategies to strengthen tough conversations. Key points of Chapter 6 are creating flow time and having people leave the conversation satisfied because they were heard. Giving all parties a voice is a key concept in this tool.

"Tool #7: Don't Say "Utilize" illustrates the power of choosing the appropriate vocabulary level and style for the audience and topic being covered. Realizing that a high percentage of human communication is nonverbal, matching body language with the intent of the conversation is key. Using "two-bit" rather than "two-buck" words, along with avoiding common conversation stoppers, will also be examined in Chapter 7.

"Tool #8: Position Power, the Less You Use It, the Greater Your Power Becomes" introduces how to build a 2 + 2 = 5 Team. Funny math? I know. But, when we work together, our sum is greater than our parts. In this chapter, we explore questions like: "What factors need to be in place to create a 2 + 2 = 5 environment?" "How do we empower leaders to grow personal power to the point it exceeds positional power?" and, "How do leaders build trust so that their team feels comfortable being honest with them?" The impact of humor in building a 2 + 2 = 5 team is also explored.

"Tool #9: Addressing the Negative Impacts of Stress on the Team" explores challenges and solutions for managing emotional weather systems within a team. I also discuss different sources of stress and how to support individuals and the team as a whole as they navigate the issues, both at work and in their personal lives. The section on "Leading During Times of Trauma" offers strategies for dealing with the team and the entire community during the information and healing process.

"Tool #10: Your Health as a Leader - Oxygen Masks and Starfish Throwers" begins by exploring those difficult times when a leader feels lonely and vulnerable, and shares insights on how to navigate and celebrate those difficult times. This chapter also explores those awkward times when a leader makes a mistake or says something that turns out to be inaccurate. Because the emotional health of the leader is crucial to serving the team, Chapter 10 also shares strategies for self-care for the leader. Human joy can come from sharing emotional experiences with others— and leaders need to experience that joy too. Leaders should be heartened by the fact that whether the experiences are positive celebrations or somber occasions, shared events can provide joy, build trust, and create confidence in the leader. The final section of Chapter 10 focuses on building a team culture of caring.

The ten tools summarized on the previous pages are all about building, strengthening, and sustaining those strong trust bridges that will be crucial to improving communication in every part of our lives. Each chapter and story explores a different set of strategies and examples for a specific focus area. When the tools are combined together as a whole unit, they create a detailed and versatile road map for navigating and succeeding in a broad range of situations.

Throughout the book, I emphasize that building trust bridges will take time. Gluing together a bridge, one stick at a time with another human being requires patience and persistence. I encourage you to be patient with yourself as you learn and try strategies that are new. Considering and actually trying new ideas and approaches will bring the growth and positive results we all strive for in our personal and professional lives.

CHAPTER 1

TOOL #1: SOLVE IT–DON'T WIN IT

Solve It–Don't Win It (SIDWI) is an attitude. It is a belief. It's an intentional way to deal with hard issues and treat people with respect in the process. Colloquialisms like: "my way or the highway," "all or nothing," "I know what is best," or "because I told you so" give one person all the power in a situation, and such phrases do not allow for any deviation or compromise in the conversation. But, there is another way, a *better* way.

Switching tactics from traditional power approaches, like those listed above, to SIDWI can be scary. But SIDWI is a choice. It's the decision to share power with others and to create a setting that encourages a shared outcome. Such an outcome is usually found in the grey area, where both participants feel satisfied with the outcome. Some leaders might only try SIDWI as a last resort, in a stalemate, or when the stakes are too high to risk an "all or nothing" outcome. There is a higher risk by not using SIDWI. Failure to use this tool with family, in the workplace, or in life may result in winning the battle, but also may result in losing the relationship with a child, student, colleague, or team.

The good news is, when you become familiar and skilled at using SIDWI, barriers come down, trust grows, and bridges are built. Those bridges become strong enough to carry the most precious cargo—your relationships with your family, friends, and teammates.

The Basic Steps of Using SIDWI to Build a Trust Bridge

The following steps of SIDWI take the reader through an emotional conference from beginning to end, using concrete details, a script, and various
techniques to diffuse emotions. Each step adds a drop of glue to the trust
bridge. At each step, I share the rationale for the inclusion of the strategy
and word choices.

In the table below, I outline the basic three steps of SIDWI (see Table
1.1). Although each situation is unique, grounding conversations with these
three steps in mind, creates a space where both parties feel heard and where
developing solutions is the focus rather than declaring a "winner." Since
compromise is at the heart of SIDWI, these three steps are key to establishing
an atmosphere where nobody in the room is digging in their heels.

Table 1.1.
Key Steps in Solve It Don't Win It

Step 1	Listening	Setting up the first steps of the trust bridge; paying attention to first impressions (i.e. body language, tone, volume); controlling the pace of the meeting
Step 2	Learning	Taking notes; planning comments and actions to take; compromising; creating positive momentum
Step 3	Leading	Taking a break; transferring power, moving into the grey area to share thoughts; leading the conversation to build a bridge between the parties.

Note: In this table, readers learn about the basic steps of SIDWI. For more specific
information refer to the examples in the paragraphs and sections that follow.

The steps outlined in Table 1.1 emphasize coming up with a solution that both parties can agree on. In step 1, "Listening", the focus is on concrete steps that decrease emotions and begin building trust. Beginning the conversation using appropriate body language, and controlling the tone, volume, and pace are all included in this step. Step 2, "Learning", involves noting possible comments or actions that might be used later to build the trust bridge. Strategies for transferring power and moving into the grey area of compromise include *kissing the ring* and *giving them their day in court*. Building positive momentum and using words that invite the concerned parties into the grey area will be a focus of this step. Step 3, "Leading", begins after taking a brief break. This step focuses on transferring power and sharing thoughts about the situation. The previous steps included being a careful, patient listener, waiting your turn, defusing and honoring emotions, and in Step 3, leading the conversation to its bridge-building conclusion. By not responding to negative body language, asking clarifying questions, and thoughtfully considering the answers, you can keep positive momentum, and end the meeting with a strong start toward building a trust bridge.

Step 1: Listening

Preparing the emotional and physical environment is a key part of the first step of SIDWI. Providing a safe, comfortable space to share is an essential part of building the trust bridge. As you walk them into the room, take a deep breath and remember to focus on the emotions in the room. Remember that much of human communication is nonverbal. Be thinking about body language—both yours and theirs. Ask yourself, "What is my face doing?" and "What is their face doing?" Be prepared with water bottles or a pitcher of water and say, "I'm going to have a glass of water, can I get you one, too?" At this early point, you might be a little emotional and stressed, so concentrate on speaking slowly and in a quiet voice. Sit across the table, giving both you and the other person a safe physical space.

Be prepared with a notepad and ask, "Is it ok if I take notes?" This shows respect and demonstrates that you care about what they are going to say. When they say, "Yes," you're now in control of the pace in a positive way. As they pick up speed, you'll say in a soft voice and gesture with your hand, "Whoa! Whoa! still writing." Fill up the first page on the notepad as quickly as possible, skipping lines and making arrows and side notes. This will send the message that you're listening carefully and getting down every word. When turning the first page, pick up the notepad in one hand, and holding the pad, grab the page by the corner and rattle it loudly as you fold it behind the notepad. I call this technique "rattling the tablet". The meeting participants love it— they know you're hearing their input and doing your best to record their every word.

Step 2: Learning

Purposely let the other party talk first. This allows them to start to feel some power and begin to relax. When they speak, lean in, make as much eye contact as possible, and nod slowly as you write. As they talk, you're learning. At this point, you're taking note of any possible baby steps you might use later when trying to move toward an emotional compromise. Continue to let them know, through positive, nonverbal cues, that you are listening intently and care about what they are sharing. Stay patient and take your time so they don't feel rushed. You're honoring their feelings by not interrupting and by hearing them out.

Kissing the ring is now a figure of speech, but the saying is based on the tradition of humility, respect, and honor for someone in power, such as royalty or a dictator. By treating the partner in your conversation with respect during steps 1 and 2, they experience humility, respect, and honor similar to someone in power. The high emotions felt at the beginning of the session have probably lessened, and their body language may have become more relaxed and positive. Some early stages of trust building are beginning, but more time and Elmer's trust glue will still be needed to strengthen this new bridge.

Part of your ability to stay calm and positive under attack comes from entering into the session with the expectation it will be tough and emotional. Again, you only interrupt to ask clarifying questions or to ask them to slow down. Giving them their "day in court" reinforces the transfer of power that will happen in steps 2 and 3. Remember that liking them personally or agreeing with what they say is not necessary for this step to be successful. Stay patient and remain willing to continue listening carefully, and taking notes in order to get the bridge started. Only after they have completed their thoughts will you speak.

At some point, they may invite you onto the trust bridge by asking your opinion, or they may just finish sharing their views on the issue. Say, "Thanks so much for sharing with me. I need to use the restroom now. Let's take a five-minute break." This break gives them time to realize they have been shown respect, and they have been given the opportunity to express all of the thoughts they came to share.

In addition to learning about where they were coming from, allowing them to share their story first adds even more sticks and glue to the bridge. The fact that you didn't overreact when you may have disagreed with them adds more glue and potential goodwill as you both move toward a mutually agreeable solution. In their mind, you have now earned your turn to speak, and they should be more open to listening to you.

Step 3. Leading

When returning to the room after the break (at the conclusion of step 2), offer them a water refill. If they don't have a notepad and pen, ask them if they want one. Lean slightly forward and keep firm, but not fierce, eye contact. Speak slowly and in a quiet voice. Nod affirmatively and smile slightly while keeping close track of their body language. Don't take the bait if they frown or tense up, but if you notice these visual cues, tone down your body language, especially the smiling, to suit the tone of the conversation. The trust bridge you're building is fragile, and you don't want to risk the participants misreading a smile as a smirk, as being sarcastic, or as taking them lightly.

Keep moving ahead, reminding yourself that you are the person who is now in the driver's seat in the situation. You've already planned to share your power by heading into the grey area, that area between their my-way-or-the-highway demands and an acceptable conclusion that can work for all parties involved. Building a new bridge requires care and patience. Don't try to build the entire bridge with one statement—or even in one meeting. Remember, the Golden Gate Bridge took years to build, and some bridges begin only one lane at a time, so stay patient. The only way to build a bridge strong enough to handle strong emotions is one stick at a time.

Continue to use positive body language and words, and keep inviting them to stay engaged. If their face turns quizzical when you share a point of view, pause and clarify. You might say, "No, that's not exactly what I meant" or rephrase what you just said. Encourage and remind them to ask questions if they don't understand. Don't move on until they're clear about each point. This patience brings them into the grey area as co-owners of any solutions. When there is an opening, ask, "So are you thinking _____ might be part of a solution?" or "Can you think of any small things that might help us here?"

After you've shared your thoughts and answered their questions, suggest another break. Say something like: "This is a lot to chew on," "There are a lot of pieces to this puzzle," or "Let's give ourselves some flow time on this" (see Chapter 7 for more on "flow time"). With this final comment, you have reminded them that their concerns are important and worthy of your thoughtful consideration— and that you didn't enter the meeting with a solution already in mind. This comment also sends them the clear message that you are co-pilots on this journey, and they are expected to continue to work on potential solutions during the break.

How much flow time depends on the urgency of the issues. Ask yourself: "Is someone in physical danger now?" "Does a decision need to be made on a timeline?" or "Are we talking about opinions and philosophies that could be dealt with in the future?" Whether the break is ten minutes, until lunch, the following week, or until a time to be determined later, make sure to meet the agreed upon commitments by carefully following through. Accurate, timely follow through is an important bridge-builder. Finally, make sure to send handwritten thank-you notes to those involved in the meeting. This small gesture goes a long way to building trust and respect.

Learning How to Use SIDWI

The first 18 years of my career were at a high school of 1,200-1,500 students with a staff of about 125. For six years, I was a classroom teacher in geometry, biology and English, as well as head varsity baseball coach. I believed I had the answers and the power in my classroom and on the baseball field. I worked hard to build strong trust bridges with my students and players, and almost all issues were solved the way I saw fit. In a nutshell, things seemed to be going pretty well for the students, the players, and myself.

In my seventh year, however, I became a full-time counselor and quickly realized that I had no power. For the next twelve years, with the responsibility of working with a group of 400 students assigned to me, I spent my days learning how to deal with all kinds of problems. On any given day, I found myself mediating conflicts between students, teachers and students, students and their parents, one or more teachers, teachers and administrators, two or more coaches, or parents with coaches and/or teachers. It was during my twelve years as a counselor that most of the ideas and the convictions that are in this book were formed.

Using SIDWI to Navigate Conflicts as a Counselor

Most of my counseling time was spent with families in crisis. Many times, I had knowledge of the families due to experiences with older siblings. Emotions for involved parties (i.e. parents, teachers, students, coaches, or administrators) were often at a fever pitch by the time the issue reached my desk. The my-way-or-the-highway approach I had used during my first six years of teaching and coaching did not work in these emotionally charged counseling sessions. I saw my old power approaches lead to setbacks and even worse in some counseling situations. I knew I had to change. So out of frustration and a feeling of failure, I developed SIDWI, a new approach, a "win-win" approach for the students and families I worked with. In the following example, I share an experience I had using SIDWI with a student and his family while working as a school counselor many years ago.

Ryan and His Family in Crisis. My session with Ryan* (all names throughout this book have been changed to pseudonyms) and his mom was one of the toughest I encountered as a counselor. He was a handsome, popular kid; the best athlete in the junior class, with a pretty, head cheerleader, senior girlfriend. Ryan was the youngest of four kids in a middle-class family, all of whom had attended our high school. Unfortunately for Ryan, all three of his siblings had been valedictorians at the school, and Ryan's parents expected the same high marks from their youngest child. Even though Ryan had good attendance and was not a discipline problem in his classes, school was difficult for him. Ryan worked hard and did extra credit to earn a 2.5 GPA his sophomore year; he was obviously not following in his valedictorian siblings' footsteps. Even so, his parents insisted he retake sophomore geometry during his junior year due to the C- he earned in the course as a sophomore.

Ryan was sobbing when he came into my office before school that Wednesday morning. He told me that mid-term grades had been sent home the day before, and he had another 2.5 GPA, including a C in the geometry course he was repeating with a classroom full of sophomores, most of whom were earning A's and B's. At the dinner table the night before, Ryan's father had matter-of-factly reminded him that he was an "Armstrong," and that "Armstrongs" didn't take driver's education or earn their driver's license until they had at least a 3.0 GPA. Ryan was so frustrated that he wanted to withdraw from school and move to Montana to live with his aunt and uncle.

I called his mom and asked her if she and her husband could come right up to the school to meet with Ryan and me. Because I thought the conference would be emotional, I arranged for us to meet in a larger, more soundproof room than my office. We used the larger room to provide more space and a level of physical separation. I prepared for Ryan's mother's arrival by placing bottled waters, notepads, pens, and a box of tissues on the large table. I stood up to greet her when she walked in. Her face was red as she explained that her husband was out of town that morning and would not be joining us. Ryan's chin was on his chest, and he sobbed softly with a tissue in his hand.

In a steady voice, and with firm eye contact, a soft smile, and a slight affirmative nod, I said, "Thanks for coming up on such short notice. Would you like water and something to write with?" She abruptly said, "No thanks." I sat at the end of the table; Ryan's mom sat on the same side of the table as Ryan, about 5-6 feet away from him. She looked at Ryan and said loudly, "What have you done now?" I immediately began to speak, and when she finally made eye contact with me, I continued. I calmly, quietly shared what Ryan had told me that morning, including wanting to move to Montana. In a quivering, but loud voice, she immediately advised me, "Mr. Amend, in the Armstrong family, our kids need to earn a 3.0 GPA to take driver's ed., and Ryan hasn't done that." At that point, I felt this conversation might go better with Ryan in another room, so I asked her, "Is it ok with you if Ryan steps out of the room?" and she said, "Yes."

With Ryan across the hall waiting in my office, she continued, "This is a firm rule in our house, and my husband and I aren't going to start bending our rules now for Ryan. He just needs to get the job done in his classes." I asked if I could move over and sit by her to share some information on Ryan's school records, and she said, "Of course." We looked at the transcript of Ryan's grades. Since middle school, his grades had never been above a C in math, and most of his other academic classes were C's as well. On the back of the transcript, his test scores were in the 50th-60th percentile range every year. There was even a note that his 4th grade teacher had suggested he be considered for some special education classes, but the family had declined. She reached for the tissue box and silently looked at the records as her eyes welled with tears.

I listened carefully and took notes as she began to share stories about Ryan's academic struggles in school. I gave her all the time she needed to share how she and her husband needed to "play hardball" and not change their family rules. As parents, they had never supported Ryan's feelings of inadequacy and rejection when he could never match up to his older siblings. Even so, I could see her hardened edges softening as she continued to talk about her youngest child. When I asked her to talk about some of Ryan's strengths, she described his natural leadership and popularity with his peers. Several of his youth sports coaches had commented how coachable he was and what a great kid he was to have on the team.

I didn't always agree with her. I often wanted to jump in and share my thoughts, but I resisted. I decided that in her stressed, emotional state, now was not the time to confront her about why they hadn't checked into the special education support offered to Ryan in his early years of school. I chose not to ask her directly what story Ryan's school transcripts or test scores over the years told; after all, the pattern of his average grades and his 50-60th percentile ranking on standardized tests did not indicate that he would become a more successful student in the more rigorous high school environment. I also resisted the urge to confront their insensitivity about Ryan's feelings when being compared to his siblings. I saved these, and other thoughts for a later session, if things didn't go well.

She'd talked for almost an hour when I finally sensed that she was finished sharing. Her voice quieted, and I read her body language— an anguished face, slumped shoulders, and bowed head. It told me that she would appreciate some help. I asked if she'd like to hear what I was thinking, and she said, "Yes, please." I decided to be direct with her. I shared that I thought Ryan was making a solid effort in school and that he should be allowed to get his driver's license as early as possible. Also, I shared my hope that both parents would remind Ryan that they loved him for who he is, and they should back up those words by focusing on Ryan's strengths and successes. I offered to meet with her and her husband at their convenience if they had any questions or if I could help in any way in the future. That afternoon, I sent home a letter thanking her for our meeting and outlining the key points that we had covered, including my recommendations and my offer to help at any time in the future.

There were no additional problems with Ryan during the remainder of his high school years. He aced his driver's ed. class, and his parents began responding to Ryan in a loving, supportive way, focusing on his strengths and celebrating his successes. In fact, after graduation Ryan gravitated to the hospitality industry and currently owns and operates a large, successful restaurant in town. He is a trusted leader in the community, and his own children are college graduates in successful careers. His parents are very proud of him.

Using SIDWI to Solve Adult Conflicts

In my counseling role, I also spent time mediating conflicts between adults in my building. I quickly learned adults don't fight as fair as the kids, and some adults hold grudges. I often dealt with parents, and on rare occasions, I even became the go-between for conflicts with multiple administrators in my own building. Dealing with adult staff issues from my counseling position was a key time of growth for me. The positive impact of being willing to listen without interrupting, sharing power, and agreeing in advance that the solution would come by compromising, usually allowed the necessary bridges to be built.

Because SIDWI was such a successful tool for me as a counselor, when I began to grow in my career as a principal, and eventually as a superintendent, I continued to hone my SIDWI skills through practice and application. In the following sections, I share stories of how SIDWI helped me solve problems as a district administrator. These examples share how SIDWI worked during difficult situations with parents and when negotiating contracts and budgets. Each of these instances gave me practice using SIDWI principles in new situations, testing its flexibility.

She's Coming in Hot. After four years as a building principal, three years at a middle school and one year at a high school, I was promoted to become the superintendent of a rural school district with 1,000 students. Each time I moved to a higher position of responsibility, I wondered if SIDWI would continue to work in my new role and in my new environment. In this small school district, the answer was still yes. When it came time to hire a high school principal to replace myself, I knew exactly who I wanted. I had known Mike for almost 20 years. He had been a hall of fame coach and administrator in a nearby district of 30,000 students and had earned a reputation for loving kids. Mike was known for establishing strong student and staff discipline environments wherever he'd worked. He was also a highly regarded, no-nonsense, basketball official, even at the Division I college level. His body language on the court said it all— "Don't even." We talked during his interview about how our two differing leadership styles needed to mesh and complement each other in order for us to succeed.

We learned a lot from each other over our eight years together. I frequently tiptoed into the grey area with Mike to find the best outcome possible, and he did the same with me. Mike's staff at the high school loved his firm discipline approach with students, but some weren't always sure they appreciated it when his approach was applied to them. Staff members said Mike became softer and I became tougher through our relationship. Our trust bridge was tested a few times, but after each test, the bridge became stronger. People called us "ham and eggs" and "good cop-bad cop."

Our offices were on opposite sides of the road, about a block apart. On multiple occasions over the eight years, Mike called me, and I could tell by the tense tone in his voice what was coming. "Sue Smith (or Doug Fisher or Mary White or any number of names) is on her way down, and she/he will be *coming in hot."* My staff and I could hear the gravel spinning as Sue's pick-up swung into the parking lot. After a brief greeting, my administrative assistant and business manager directed the angry parent toward my office, and I started SIDWI. A successful outcome depended on using all of the SIDWI steps to come up with a solution that worked for Mike, the parent, and for myself. And, the outcome of these meetings usually accomplished just that.

Using SIDWI to Negotiate. School bargaining is driven largely by factors that negotiators have little or no control over. School staffing accounts for more than 80% of the district's budget, and the dollars available are controlled by the legislature and local voters. Other factors influencing the school budget include: student enrollment, community demographics, and property taxes. Because of these pre-set pieces of the budget, both teams come to the table with at least some feel for the parameters. Even in such polarized bargaining situations, trust bridges can be built with a SIDWI approach, one popsicle stick at a time. Though group contract issues can be different from personal counseling situations, high emotions and the determination to reach an agreement are usually present in both circumstances. I found the same basic SIDWI counseling tenets of listening to build trust, transferring power, and moving into the grey area to be just as effective when approaching contract issues as they were when dealing with personal issues.

By nature, most contract negotiations are set up to be adversarial, and the impact of body language can be huge, especially when cameras record many bargaining sessions. Even one outward display of body language can reveal emotions present within the team. Teams often assign members not at the table to record and report on any revealing body language from the opposition and a relaxed face with a slight smile and the appropriate use of humor can help keep emotions on a more even keel. The SIDWI rule of managing emotions with a slow, steady pace and calm voice definitely holds true when bargaining. Emotions can become difficult to manage when teams harbor long-standing grudges or negative feelings about members of the opposing team. It's also common for one or both teams to enter bargaining with the feeling they got the short end of the stick at the last session, and feeling a need to make up for that with an even tougher stance on issues in this negotiation cycle.

The setting for a bargaining session should be a room at a neutral site that is well ventilated and able to seat both teams at one table. An additional room should be nearby for teams to caucus, or meet in private. Additional seating around the perimeter of the room should be available for spectators, members of the media, legal advisors, or research staff. The table should be a rectangle, five to six feet wide and long enough to seat six to ten people along each side. Veteran negotiators say, "If you can smell their breath, or if they can spit on you, the table's too narrow." Team members should be able to move around the room to have sidebar conversations or form smaller groups for private conversations.

Both teams start out with a set of written expectations. Depending on the people at the bargaining table, some sessions start with a my-way-or-the-highway approach. As is true in a tough one-on-one conversation, allowing the other team to speak first will affirm respect and trust while allowing you to learn while listening and taking notes. I frequently rattle the tablet as I write pages and pages of notes. Accurate, detailed notes—that include direct quotes—can have an impact in any counseling or bargaining process. Another way to affirm trust and gain mutual respect is to allow the opposing team to write the first draft of the proposed contract. Without exception, I have seen this approach build trust and goodwill at the table. I have also seen teams come in with lower demands than I would have been willing to settle for.

Common ground and shared values can often lead to the perceived win-win agreements present in SIDWI conversations. Everybody at the table will agree that core values, such as staff and student safety, mutual respect, and what is best for the kids, are important. Conversations about shared core values set the stage for both sides to tiptoe into the grey area. Nobody loses face when they are discussing student and staff safety. Other issues I have negotiated successfully with the SIDWI approach are attendance boundaries, school site selection, sex education, book selection, budget priorities, and personnel issues.

The final step in a SIDWI-based bargaining session is a contract written with shared power, win-win solutions, and respect for all parties. Written reports should not contain words that anger or demean the opposition. The writer should not try to get in the last word or have some kind of a parting shot. As is covered further in Chapter 6, you may not be able to please everyone, but you can treat everyone with respect and positive regard.

Conclusion

Being a patient listener, sharing power, and focusing on win-win solutions are the building blocks to creating the trust bridges necessary to solve issues. SIDWI leads off this book because it has been one of the most useful tools to me throughout my career as a counselor and administrator. Because this tool builds the foundation for connecting with any type of person in a positive way, SIDWI drives the other nine tools that follow in the book. SIDWI is a sure way of building and strengthening the crucial human trust bridges that every leader needs to succeed.

In this chapter, special care was given to provide the concrete details necessary to learn and use SIDWI, including specific verbiage and actions to take during each step. I've shared examples from interpersonal experiences and broader applications of the tool. In the following table, I have provided an action plan for using SIDWI (see Table 1.2). The action plan includes takeaways from the chapter, strategies you want to improve, and a plan to use SIDWI in your professional or personal life. Please take the time to complete this table and consider how you could use the steps of SIDWI that you've learned in this chapter.

Table 1.2
Action Plan: Solve It... Don't Win It

What are two takeaways from this section?
1.
2.
What two strategies will you use to improve your SIDWI skills?
1.
2.
What steps will you take now? (Action Step for SIDWI)

Note: This table provides readers with a place to apply what they have learned about the SIDWI strategies focused on during Chapter 1.

CHAPTER 2

TOOL #2: LEAVE THE SLEDGEHAMMER
IN THE PICKUP TRUCK

Tool #2 tests the skill level, integrity, and compassion of the user. This chapter uses the hammer analogy to decide which approach to use in a conversation. "Leave the Sledgehammer in the Pickup Truck" is about preserving people's dignity by choosing to use the right sized hammer to get the job done. When selecting a hammer for a conversation, the challenge is to select the smallest possible hammer that still gets the job done for the situation at hand. Choosing a smaller hammer may mean learning a new skill or taking more time to get the job done with the least possible collateral damage, and smaller hammer approaches always promotes kindness rather than bullying.

The chapter is organized into sections that will describe the difference between particular hammers and selecting the right hammer. The first section discusses the different types of figurative hammers. Readers explore various hammers, including their sizes and uses. Then, readers analyze which hammer is most appropriate for a particular situation and why. Readers will be asked to think about the following questions:

- Am I more experienced with a certain kind of hammer?

- Which hammer is the best size for this job?

- What is the smallest hammer I can use, and still get this job done?

- What damage will happen if I use a hammer that's too big?

Then readers will compare leader behaviors to various hammer sizes and consider some suggestions for how to approach different kinds of issues they may encounter. The final section focuses on working with people who are in crisis or marginalized in some way, and selecting a hammer size that fits with the emotional condition of that person.

Differences Between Particular Hammers

There are more than 40 types of hammers used in construction and other manufacturing activities today. Though some hammers are now pneumatic, most still rely on human "horsepower" and skills. Remodeling contractors often have a variety of hammers in their pickups. What separates a true expert craftsman from an inexperienced hacker is their ability to select, and skillfully operate, the right hammer for each part of their project. I've seen experienced contractors, with multiple hammers already in their toolbox, purchase, rent, or even borrow a hammer for a specific, tough situation that comes up on their job. For example, when a skilled craftsman first assesses a remodel project on an older home, they might make a mental list of which hammers they need. Only a hacker attempts to use a finishing hammer for demolition, or a sledgehammer to work on a 100-year old fireplace mantle. If part of the job requires a skill they don't have, the skilled contractor either learns how to do the task or brings in someone who has the needed expertise. The contractor's ability to select and use just the right hammer at just the right time determines the success of the project.

As human bridges are built or strengthened, hammer sizes may need to be adjusted. Remember to keep the hammer size in sync with the body language, attitudes, and emotions of the conversation. Changing hammer sizes may bring the surprise or shock value needed to reach the goal of a conversation. When building trust bridges, selecting the right hammer—by both people—produces familiarity, skill level, confidence, and success.

The following table shares a list of common hammers used in construction (see Table 2.1). This list will help with the discussion and Table 2.2 later in the chapter. Again, the analogy here is between contractor's hammers and matching the leader's figurative hammer selection with the emotional state and physical skill sets of the person they are working with. At the same time, every conversation has a goal, and the selected hammer must be strong enough to achieve the desired outcome, but small enough not to damage the bridge being built.

Table 2.1
Alphabetical List of Common Hammers and Their Purpose

Common Hammers
<ul><li>Ball Peen—used for shaping metal and rounding metal edges on bumps, corners etc.</li><li>Claw—probably the most recognized hammer and the first hammer that most hackers buy—the curved claw enables pulling out nails, and the smooth, flat head makes it useable in many basic functions</li><li>Club—a small version of the sledge hammer, used for light demolition and for driving steel chisels and mason heads</li><li>Framing—similar to the claw, but with a waffled head that prevents slippage when driving nail heads, the waffle pattern formed in the indented board is later covered up, usually by drywall or siding, during the completion of the construction, so the dent cannot be seen in the final product</li><li>Rip—for ripping apart materials during demolition</li><li>Roofing—for removing and applying roofing materials</li><li>Rubber—for softer blows, gentle enough to force plasterboard into place without damaging it</li><li>Sledge—heavy, large, violent blows, can break up wood, concrete masonry, popular demolition tool—requires repair and clean-up</li><li>Trim (finishing)—smaller, often tiny, smooth head, reaches small areas, won't damage wood, is not sufficient for heavier jobs</li></ul>

Note: The list of hammers above includes some of the most common types of hammers a skilled contractor might have in his pickup truck.

Choosing the Right Hammer

There are stakes involved with succeeding or failing in a conversation. Sometimes the success or failure of the team is on the line. The outcome often depends on whether the correct hammer was used. For example, when a figurative sledgehammer is used to deal with others, it can become an aggressive, power-based strategy. When using a sledgehammer in a conversation, the emotional needs and strengths of the other party are not being considered— the desired outcome of the conference becomes more important than preserving the relationship. Being unable to repair or rebuild a damaged relationship resulting from this approach must be weighed as a risk when choosing the sledgehammer. But, sometimes a sledgehammer approach is necessary. For example, if time is of the essence (i.e. a child is in danger) or if the relationship is already too damaged to repair, a sledgehammer might be the right tool. On the other hand, a small, finishing hammer is used for delicate jobs where the risk of causing a lasting negative impact on the other person (or the relationship) is too great. However, it should be noted that if the finishing hammer fails to get the job done, using a larger hammer afterward can sometimes cause more emotional pain than if the larger hammer had been used in the first place. Therefore, diagnosing which hammer to bring to a particular situation is an essential skill.

In the following section, I provide elaboration on key points shared in the table that follows. For each hammer, I give specific examples of how it could be used in human bridge-building. (See Table 2.2 for some of the common hammers along with strategies and suggestions of when to use each.)

Table 2.2
Types of Hammers and Strategies to Use

Type of Hammer	Strategy to Use	Situation for Hammer
Sledge— heavy, large, powerful, destroys or removes objects	Leader dominates, forces outcome, leader ok with starting over if necessary	Major discipline, or redirection of attitude, urgent need, or safety issue
Club—drives steel chisels and mason heads, necessary to create heavy, foundational strength	Enough force to move other key leaders who may be strong-willed. Leader allows input for pros and cons, but this is a must win conversation. Keeps them mentally and emotionally whole, and with you	Force meets force, at the beginning, Buy-in may be gradual, eventual use of smaller hammer for final resolution may occur
Ball Peen—used for shaping metal and rounding metal edges on bumps and corners, requires a strong skill set by the leader.	Clear statement affirming the person's professional strengths. Clear direction is given on where improvement is needed to move toward excellence	The person feels competent and satisfied in their work products. They will be required to improve the final products they have been producing.
Rip— rip apart materials during demolition	Explain the need for the change to produce greater success with the outcome	Initial firmness or harshness with a clear plan for a stronger, more positive result
Claw—Framing and Roofing — versatile, prepares the project, then completes the process with a stronger, more desirable outcome	Careful explanation of why the preparation steps (improvements) will strengthen the person and the team	Person has strong potential, but needs to change specific behaviors or skill levels to perform at an acceptable level

Rubber Hammer— for softer blows, gentle enough to force plaster-board into place without damaging it, requires a strong skill set by the leader	A soft, but firm tone and approach will be used here. The required change will need to happen in a timely manner. The quality of the project will depend on the person being able to carry out the task.	Like the ball peen, the person is a valued team member, but they are satisfied with adequate, but not excellent job performance. Needs an attitude adjustment to work toward the highest quality possible and not settling for anything but their best effort.
Trim (finishing)— smaller, often tiny, smooth head, reaches small areas, won't damage wood, is not sufficient for heavier jobs, requires strong skill set by the leader	Requires an even softer, counseling tone than the rubber hammer. The softest of SIDWI skills such as a quiet, slowly paced voice, and early careful listening, will allow the person to get, and keep their emotions under control enough to get the most out of the conversation the leader needs to have with them.	This team member may be a superstar supporter (i.e. very sensitive, caring, quiet, and cares deeply about other team members). Though the team member supports teammates in the most difficult of times, he/she may withdraw, rather than argue or defend themself. Needs to feel empowered and know the boss has confidence in their abilities.

Note: The table above lists common hammer types, uses, and the metaphor for the type of leadership each hammer entails.

Heavy hammers. Heavier hammers are used to solve discipline issues, modify behavior, or emphasize non-negotiable team foundations such as safety rules. There are a variety of big hammers to choose from, including the sledgehammer and club hammer.

To expand on the analogy, when addressing safety issues, the leader should select a sledgehammer. The sledgehammer approach relies on a stern, firm, direct tone, which sends the message, "I mean business," "This is serious," or "You better pay attention here." In many industries such as construction, manufacturing, and energy, employees sign an affidavit to affirm they have received and understand the safety training. The sledgehammer approach is obvious— if the employee disobeys the safety rules, they may lose their job, suffer physical injury, or even die.

When I worked as a school principal, I also had to use the sledgehammer during various discipline scenarios. During these meetings, my body language included a neutral face, firm eye contact, and erect, forward-leaning posture. These nonverbal messages made it clear that I was in control of the conversation, and the other person would speak if, or when, I allowed. As these difficult conversations often ended with some form of discipline or firm directive, I did not soften the impact of the meeting by talking about something else. It was not the time to talk about their children, their accomplishments or the barbecue the other night. I made sure they walked out of the door of my office knowing exactly what my message had been.

The club hammer, which drives the steel chisels and mason heads necessary to create heavy, foundational strength, is another hammer to choose when items are non-negotiable. Unlike the sledge, the club hammer does not carry a negative or punitive connotation. When the club hammer comes out, the verbal and nonverbal language of the leader is positive and encouraging because the user brings strength and improvement to the team. The example of a dentist's drill, where the patient realizes the required pain will be worth the gain, is an analogy to the club hammer. Humor can often be used with this hammer, and a feeling of "We're all in this together" and "This will really be worth it when the job is done" usually prevails. I was able to use club hammer strategies when parts of a construction project needed to take place while students and staff were in the building. At these disruptive times, I used humor while firmly describing the increased safety and security that was necessary. In this setting, I took time to recognize and support the team members whose daily routines were most severely impacted during the project. Attendance at these meetings was strictly enforced, and people were required to sign in when they entered the room. I always followed up by providing written notes of the meeting, thus eliminating any chance of misinterpretation and lessening the impact of poor note-taking by any team members.

Daily hammers. Rip, claw, framing, and roofing hammers are important analogies for several reasons. These hammers represent the daily grind present in most jobs. The use of these smaller hammers in establishing and maintaining a daily work ethic is almost always accompanied by an upbeat, positive smile and encouraging words. These hammers are not too heavy, but also not too light.

Many team members become educators because they want to be servant leaders. They learn that being a servant leader can be exhausting and often happens without recognition. The claw, framing, and roofing hammers can be used in conversations that include the need for improvement and reflection, while also recognizing that team member's strengths. Daily hammers may also be used when conducting evaluations. In these meetings, the leader often finds both strengths and weaknesses in the team member's job performance. These two-way conversations can build trust bridges as performance expectations are discussed along with commendations and sincere thank yous.

Lighter, smaller hammers. Small hammer strategies are used in situations where finesse is necessary to add the finishing touches to a sensitive conversation. Because finishing hammers are used to deal with delicate situations, these hammers often come into play when emotions are high or when smaller details need to be dealt with. Rubber and trim hammers also employ small hammer strategies and are largely the opposite from the heavy hammer strategies listed above.

It has often been said that great teams take care of the smallest details. The rubber hammer is used for the team member who has the ability to do the trim job, but is lacking in focus or willingness. It's their attitude and approach that need to be dealt with to successfully complete the assignment. Walking away from a task, or calling it good before the finishing steps are complete is not acceptable. The boss needs to insist that a maximum effort is made to create a final product that everyone can be proud of —in other words "to put a bow on it." When using the small hammers, words and body language are still firm, while being upbeat, encouraging, and enthusiastic.

Situations involving disappointment, frustration, conflict, or tragedy call for light, small hammers. Skilled use of rubber hammers or trim hammers, with their softer approaches, can be rewarding in several ways. With smaller hammers, people don't feel afraid— rather, they feel invited and encouraged to become an equal partner in the conversation, which builds trust. People can tell when their leaders are sensitive to their emotional needs, and are using a softer touch. SIDWI skills (Chapter 1) such as a quieter, slower voice, positive head nodding, follow-up questions and note taking, are key components in small hammer approaches. When small hammers are used for consoling, encouraging, and empowering, the words become powerful and healing to the team.

Chapter 9, *Addressing the Negative Impacts of Stress on the Team*, focuses on the use of small hammer skills when processing and healing from trauma. Lighter hammers can help develop coping skills in any team environment, because they preserve dignity, build trust, and make people feel safe. The new trust bridges, forged during difficult times, can cause all stakeholders to walk hand in hand as partners moving forward from the trauma.

Different sized hammer strategies can be used when greeting and orienting new team members. As shared earlier in this Chapter, the smaller hammers can begin building trust bridges by making the new person feel welcomed and valued. During the same conversation, larger hammer approaches can drive home the policies, procedures and protocols important to the team's success. Experience, lessons learned, and growing instincts over time are the surest ways to gain skills in selecting and successfully using different hammer approaches. As with the contractor, practice will make perfect for you. Be patient with yourself as you improve your human bridge building skills—your efforts will be worth it.

The following three stories illustrate outcomes experienced by children and adolescents when subjected to different hammer sizes. "Even a Seven-Year-Old Can Recognize Bullying" and "Jerry" both describe situations where a sledgehammer was used directly and harshly. In neither situation was any attempt made by the bully to heal or repair the damage caused by their use of the sledgehammer. The witnessing of the use of a sledgehammer in "Even a Seven-Year-Old Can Recognize Bullying" had a lifelong impact on a young boy. Jerry was stunned and heartbroken when he was blindsided by his new step-father. The healing in Jerry's heart was enhanced by caring people outside of his family who rallied to support him in his time of need. In the "Senior Boys English" account, every hammer size was used over the 180-day school year. Each day, the needs of the young men in my classroom called for using different hammers. By far the most common hammers were the daily hammers (i.e. rip, claw, framing, and roofing hammers). Those hammers were capable of getting and maintaining the attention of those young men while still building the trust bridges necessary to lead them to graduation and success in life.

Even a Seven-Year-Old Can Recognize Bullying

Six days a week during the summer of 1952, my mom packed a peanut butter and jelly sandwich and some carrot sticks for my brother Dexter and me and sent us out the door. We walked a mile down a dirt road with our baseball gloves to the segregated community center. The complex had several baseball fields, surrounded by green grass that seemed to go forever. I remember it being filled with an equal number of White and Black kids, though the Black kids couldn't use the drinking fountains or bathrooms or sit in the same area as the White kids at lunch.

That summer, my brother and I played pickup games like work-up and roll-a-bat. In roll-a-bat, the batter put the bat on the ground after hitting the ball out into the field. Kids scrambled and competed to field the batted balls, and the competition was rough and tumble. If the fielder rolled the ball in and hit the bat, he became the hitter. The rules were clear, and both Black and White kids played the game together. I couldn't understand why the Black kids never got to bat. For example, when a Black kid caught the ball and hit the bat lying on the ground, a White kid said, "You stay out here. I'm hitting!" The Black kids spent all their time in the field and none of their time at home plate hitting.

If a Black kid ever tried to stand up for himself, a group of White kids ganged up on him and beat him up, and it seemed like it always took a long time for the adult supervisor to break up the beating. One-time Dexter tried to defend a Black kid, and Dex was threatened by a mob of White kids. It always made me cry. I'd never experienced hate before, but even a seven-year-old could recognize bullying.

I selected this story from my childhood because after decades of working with, and trying to support people, I now realize that every bullying situation involves at least one bully and at least one underdog. I view all forms of bullying as the most cruel and damaging use of the sledgehammer approach. Even among adults in the workplace, whether bullying is silent or spoken, it is destructive to the people directly involved, as well as the bystanders.

Senior Boys English

It was 1969, prior to the Special Education and Title IX laws that passed in the early 1970's. It was my first year as a teacher. Over the previous summer, I'd met with my school administrators and gotten permission to design a class called "Senior Boys English." This class served the 24 boys who had the least chance of passing one of the current regular senior English classes that were required to graduate. The concept was that I would teach these boys using strategies and vocabulary that related to their lives. In this way, I could help scaffold the English content necessary to meet state graduation requirements. As part of my proposal, I offered to handle any discipline problems within my classroom rather than sending students to the office for discipline. Most of my students were "frequent fliers" in the school discipline system, so my plan not only benefited the students, but also the administrators and other English teachers. This appealed to the administration and sealed the deal for approving the class.

To meet the graduation requirements, the students were required to demonstrate reading proficiency, write a five-paragraph theme, give an oral classroom presentation, and write a research paper. I was given plenty of leeway to develop curriculum materials and classroom activities that better fit the needs of these young men. We integrated music to learn about the power of poetry (e.g. "Bridge over Troubled Waters" (Simon and Garfunkel, Columbia Records, 1970) and "Jesus Christ Superstar" (Webber and Rice producers, Decca Records, 1970). For the reading and writing parts of the curriculum, I brought in special interest periodicals and newspapers. I was even given a budget to buy paperbacks that interested the students.

As I contacted parents over the summer to get permission for their son to be in this special class, I immediately heard common threads. I listened to stories of past struggles in English. I heard that their sons "had been swimming upstream in school since kindergarten," "had older brothers and sisters who were excellent students," and "had just gone into [their] shell about English." Many parents shared emotional stories of how their son had been bullied and humiliated for "being dumb" or "not knowing how to read." Parents described how this bullying often resulted in fisticuffs, with one student having been suspended from school several times over the years for fighting with bullies. Several parents noted that even some teachers had stereotyped their sons as "poor students." These parents had tried everything to help their sons succeed, and some were already worried about having to tell relatives their son would not be graduating. I learned that, in addition to the value of a high school diploma, the symbolism of graduating was of special importance to these families.

I taught the class for six years, and for six years, each young man entered room 23 with his own life story. There were students of every range of ability, from deep mental and physical disabilities to genius IQs. Their strongest common bond was their need to pass the class to graduate. Sons of doctors, lawyers, brick masons, educators, and all levels of income and social standing in the community, were present on the first day of class every year. There was nervous laughter and joking, and I heard the same concerns that I'd heard from their parents.

They were silent as I told them about the four specific assignments they needed to complete to graduate. I reminded them we had 180 days to get it done, and that we'd be working together to make sure everyone got through. When I explained that they would choose their own topics for each of the assignments, some air began to come back into the room.

Over the course of the year, some students were amazed to learn that they actually could read when it was something they were interested in. They learned giving a speech in front of the class wasn't that scary when you could bring in your motorcycle and demonstrate how to overhaul a carburetor. I remember one sheep-shearing speech ending abruptly when the sheep broke loose and went bawling down the hall just as the lunch bell rang. One student was even elected as the senior class graduation speaker and got a standing ovation for the speech he and his classmates wrote in Senior Boys English.

Some boys were very smooth talkers, but couldn't write a paragraph. When I said, "Just write down what you are saying," they realized they may not be very good spellers, but, if they could say it, they could write it. This was a breakthrough and led to the class making their own spelling lists of words to learn. On writing assignments, I required a minimum number of words. As the year went on, it was rewarding to see some young men actually writing more than the exact number of words required.

My six years of experience with these classes, taught me one of my first and most important lessons about selecting hammers when working with people. Some days, the toughest thing for me was to control my own emotions before I picked the hammer they, and I, needed at that moment. During our 55-minute classes, I might have the urge to use a sledgehammer and a trim hammer on the same kid within a ten-minute period of time. I made a lot of mistakes choosing hammers, but I continued trying to read their emotions and intent before I reacted. I got much better. I learned not to pick a hammer when I wasn't in control of my own emotions, and I learned not to pick a hammer until I was fairly sure of their emotions and motives. Those were two, crucial hammer lessons that I still use today.

Jerry: An Innocent Victim of the Sledgehammer Approach

After arriving at school on Monday after spring vacation, I found a small, battered suitcase and a backpack in front of my office door. Soon after, a shy senior boy in my counseling group came around the corner of the hall and into my office. Jerry, an 18-year old, was a transfer student from Billings, Montana, and I didn't know him well prior to that morning. In a steady voice, he explained that the night before was his new step-dad's first night of staying in the house with Jerry and his family. As his mom and two younger sisters sat at the table with their heads down, Jerry said his step-dad had given him no warning or explanation as he demanded that Jerry pack up his things and get out of the house. No one else at the table had spoken, and Jerry said he had no idea why his step-dad had kicked him out.

In a strong voice, Jerry assured me that he had a place to stay with a friend's family until graduation, and he only needed my help for two things. Jerry asked me to hide his suitcase at the school. He didn't want his family to know that he was still attending school. Jerry also asked me to make sure the school did not contact his family about graduation, credits, or anything else. I decided to help Jerry, and he never missed a day of school the rest of the year. I checked in with him frequently, and he was always upbeat. He'd made a few good friends, got along with his teachers, and was doing fine. Jerry graduated with his class, and when I returned to my office that evening after the ceremony, his battered suitcase was gone. Later, I learned that he had moved out of state to live with relatives and attend college. I never met, nor heard from, his mother or step-dad.

I've never forgotten the harshness of Jerry's step-dad's sledgehammer approach. I think about what it must have been like for Jerry's mom and the younger siblings in the home that night. How could this man be willing to separate a young man from his family during the spring of his senior year in high school? What could possibly have pushed him to treat Jerry so harshly? Because Jerry stayed upbeat, with a quiet smile and can-do attitude, I've always marveled and wondered what made him such a strong and resilient young man.

Sledgehammers Hurt Underdogs

Each of the three stories above dealt with underdog kids who were victimized by bullies wielding figurative sledgehammers. Both Jerry and the Black kids in Charlotte lost dignity and experienced pain from the sledgehammer approach. Many of the fragile students in Senior Boys English class experienced the sad and painful impact of bullying during their childhood years. Despite their scars from being bullied, these young men were gradually able to bounce back and grow in self-confidence because of their new successes and new trust bridges built among their Senior Boys English family.

Beginning with my experiences with bullying in Charlotte as a seven-year-old and continuing throughout my life and in the field of education, I have felt a special level of concern and compassion for underdogs. I've learned that underdogs come in all shapes, sizes, ages, colors, and genders. Underdogs come from families that are rich, poor, blended, or single parent.

They come with all types of appearances, and with all levels of intelligence and motivation.

Underdogs and bullies can switch places. One year, I was sitting at a table with a bunch of my former baseball players at their 20-year class reunion when a gorgeous brunette came over and asked if she could sit down at our table. She was the only woman at the table. The players were awestruck with her beauty and the classy way in which she conducted herself. After about 20 minutes of casual conversation, she stood up to leave and one of the star players, perhaps the most well-known student in the class, said, "This is killing me. Were you in our class?" In a strong and somewhat coy voice, she answered, "Yes, Pete, but that was back when I was a '2' and you were a '10.'" As she smiled and walked away, Pete's teammates roared with laughter. 20 years ago, Pete had made fun of this young woman, but that night, she had turned the tables on him.

Underdogs of all shapes, ages and incomes. The year after retiring from education, I had the honor of serving as the first development director and staff trainer for the new, non-profit community center in our city (from 2008-2010). As individuals and businesses stepped forward, our community raised $8 million to help fund the construction and endowment of the center which was scheduled to open to 20,000 new members in the spring of 2009. As the financial crisis of 2008-2009 struck, many prominent, wealthy people temporarily became underdogs. In my office at the center, with the door closed and curtains drawn, the normally confident and powerful leaders tearfully shared they weren't able to meet their financial pledge on time. "Nothing like this has ever happened to me," they shared. Some had to lay off employees and did not know how they could make payroll in future months for the remaining employees.

Accustomed to a life of affluence, prestige, and influence, these people were as fragile and vulnerable as any underdog I had ever met at a homeless camp. Every day, I reminded our staff that people who were flying high last month might now be underdogs. It reminded me of the fragility of life— that on any day, a health diagnosis, a relationship issue, or a financial situation could make a person an underdog. One of my passions behind writing this book is helping all underdogs, no matter how they got there.

Conclusion

Why do we respond with emotion when we see, hear, and talk about underdogs and bullying? For me, my emotions are a mixed bag. My feelings are sadness, anger, and rage. But, I also have feelings of hope. I believe that people of all ages and every walk of life can learn to leave their sledgehammers in the pickup when dealing with other human beings. I believe we can learn to use sledgehammers only in the most serious of situations involving safety and discipline, and we can learn to decide to use smaller hammers on a daily basis. We can begin building the bridges of trust, respect, and caring, one small hammer stroke at a time.

I hope you will make a special effort when tackling the action plan for this chapter (see Table 2.3). Think about your own hammer patterns of dealing with other people, especially the underdogs you encounter in your life. Make a commitment to purposely try a smaller hammer than you may have used in the past.

Table 2.3
Action Plan: Leave the Sledgehammer in the Pickup Truck

What are two takeaways from this section? 1. 2.
What two strategies will you use to improve skills when selecting and using figurative hammers? 1. 2.
What steps will you take now? (Action Step for Choosing the Right Hammer)

Note: This table provides readers with a place to apply what they have learned about hammer sizes and the impact of different approaches when dealing with situations at home, at work, or any other setting.

CHAPTER 3

TOOL #3: DON'T MAJOR IN THE MINORS

"Don't Major in the Minors" focuses on the importance of prioritizing. When considering personal, family, social, and work-related responsibilities that exist on a daily basis, leaders feel like they're drinking through the proverbial fire hose. If we answered yes to every request or tried to complete every task on the day's to-do list, there literally wouldn't be enough time to complete all of those tasks in a 24-hour period. Because of the short and long-term deleterious health impacts of constant job demands, Tool #3 addresses how to manage priorities and reduce stress.

Many leadership books discuss the negative impacts of stress in the workplace. Whether the stress is a slow drip or caused by an acute crisis, the damaging health impacts can be the same. Disappointment, fear, and panic are heavy burdens for anyone to carry, and the physical and emotional strength of everyone involved is sapped. The tyranny of the urgent and the impossible expectations of a to-do list that is too long can haunt a person. By using the tools in this chapter, leaders can reduce stress for both themselves and their team. The three sections of this chapter are "Spending Time with Your Team", "The Hourglass" and "How the Leadership Filter Reduces Stress". (More information about maintaining mental and physical health for teams and leaders will be shared in Chapters 9 and 10).

Spending Time with Your Team

When I invest the time to connect with my team, I am majoring in the majors (i.e. the business version of the golf balls mentioned in "A Reflection of Life"—see Figure 3.1). I believe employees are more successful when they experience a personal connection with their leader. Regular attention from the leader validates the importance of what they are doing, and with affirmation, clarification, and correction when needed, it is the engine of higher performance. Frequent attention empowers people and can lead to trust bridges being built or strengthened. Conversely, lack of attention leads to the opposite response, even from a high performing team member.

Though connecting in person creates the strongest bridges, it's the thought that counts when a person receives a quick call, voicemail, note, email, or social media greeting. Sincere praise in front of peers is empowering and bridge-building.

The other two strategies presented in this chapter, the Hourglass and the Leadership Filter, will also help you avoid majoring in the minors. The "Hourglass" section frames the time pressure realities every leader faces in making the most out of their 24-hour day. The "Leadership Filter" explores the power a leader has to manage their stress load by carefully choosing which issues they will or will not share with others. Both sections guide readers to consider ways of prioritizing. Finally, I share some lessons I learned the hard way in the final section of the chapter.

The Hourglass

Throughout recorded history, the hourglass has been used as a precise, accurate timer. The unchangeable reality that there is a finite amount of sand that takes an exact amount of time to drain from top to bottom stares us in the face. As the top of the hourglass empties, every observer is reminded of the unavoidable reality that time is almost up. In the following section, I share tips to prioritizing your to-do list and making time for what's important. See Figure 3.1 for an allegory about prioritizing— "A Reflection on Life." Written by an unknown author, this story has been shared in many group settings, online, and in print over the years. You may also watch a video of the story on YouTube, or read an alternate version on Medium.com.

Figure 3.1
Prioritizing Your Golf Balls: A Reflection on Life

A professor stood before his philosophy class and had some items in front of him. When the class began, wordlessly, he picked up a very large, empty mayonnaise jar and proceeded to fill it with golf balls. Then, he asked the students if the jar was full. They agreed it was. The professor then picked up a box of pebbles and poured them into the jar. He shook the jar lightly. The pebbles rolled into the open areas between the golf balls. He then asked the students again if the jar was full. They agreed it was. The professor then picked up a box of sand and poured it into the jar. Of course, the sand filled up everything else. He asked once more if the jar was full.

The students responded unanimously, "Yes."

The professor then produced two cups of coffee from under the table and poured the entire contents into the jar, effectively filling the empty space between the sand. The students laughed.

"Now," said the professor, as the student's laughter subsided. "I want you to recognize that this jar represents your life. The golf balls are the important things—your God, family, children, health, friends, and favorite passions—things that if everything else was lost and only they remained, your life would still be full. The pebbles are the other things that matter like your job, house, and car. The sand is everything else, the small stuff. If you put the sand in the jar first, there would be no room for the pebbles or the golf balls. The same goes for life. If you spend all your time and energy on the small stuff, you will never have room for the things that are important to you.

"Pay attention to the things that are critical to your happiness. Play with your children. Take time to get medical check-ups. Take your special someone to dinner. Play another 18 holes of golf. There will always be time to clean the house and fix the disposal. Take care of the golf balls first, the things that really matter. Set your priorities. The rest is just sand."

One of the students raised her hand and inquired what the coffee represented.

The professor smiled. "I'm glad you asked. It just goes to show you that no matter how full your life may seem, there's always room for a couple of cups of coffee with a friend."

Note: This story was written from my memory, with a sports twist using golf balls rather than rocks.

Egg timers and managing time. I keep a three-minute, sand egg timer on my desk and have given many such timers as gifts to colleagues, family, and friends over the years. Just a glance at this egg timer is a constant visual reminder that there are exactly 24 hours in each day, and not a minute more. I cannot add more sand to this egg timer any more than I can add minutes or hours to my day. The egg timer also reminds me that if I decide to spend two extra hours on my job responsibilities, those 120 minutes subtract from my family time, my buffer time, or my sleep bank. Being at work two hours earlier or later, working weekends, or any other approach does not change the reality of the hourglass.

Calendars. Whether an electronic calendar system, a whiteboard, or a paperback planner, making use of calendars—and making sure golf ball items and major to-do list items—are on the calendar is vital. In addition to helping you get the most out of your hourglass, an accurate calendar, shared with those who live or work with you, will work wonders in allowing people to plan around your schedule.

Required meetings or appointments will always be on my calendar, but if my job requires more flexible duties such as answering emails each day, or doing random contacts with my team each day, I place my "responding to emails" and "staff contacts" time slots on my calendar for everyone to see and use for their own planning. If I choose to meet with my friend every week, or work out on a regular basis, I schedule both on my calendar, even if the meeting is after work hours. As a leader, I encourage my team to follow my lead and schedule family activities, such as barbecues, games, concerts, or other events on their calendar the same way they schedule a doctor's appointment or important business appointment. Then, if someone needs something from them during that time, they can answer, "Nope. Sorry, I'm booked."

Respecting my own time, and my team members' time, helps me to prioritize and always keep my eye on the hourglass. Disciplining myself to keep only worthy things in my hourglass is still a work in progress for me, but the better I get at controlling what ends up in my hourglass, the happier and healthier I feel. Finally, as a boss, I can use my position to support and influence the people I work with in their efforts to focus and spend time on their golf ball activities. See Table 3.1 for specific strategies for prioritizing your hourglass. The table shares detailed strategies you can use and refer back to as you continue to read this book.

Table. 3.1
Hourglass Strategies

Your Calendar

Use your calendar—always keep it handy in your phone, device, and/or binder
 	
• Every evening check your calendar for the rest of the week
 	
• Remember to check weekends too
 	
• Written calendars are huge stress relievers
 	
    ◊ Once it's on your calendar, you don't have to remember it
 	
    ◊ The structure provided by your calendar organizes your events and "forces" you to follow your own daily plan/roadmap

Write everything that takes up your time on the calendar— • Include personal and professional items • Include everything that takes up time (i.e. email responses, grading papers, writing evaluations)

Share your calendar—remember, knowledge is power and managing your calendar should be a team effort

- Over time, using your calendar will train your colleagues, family and friends about what you value most

    ◊ Be predictable

        ■ Joe never misses his kid's events

        ■ Joe won't be there on Sunday, he's got church stuff

        ■ If it's not for a good cause, Joe probably won't be there

Verbally, or electronically sync your calendar with family members and colleagues. This will allow them to—

- Adjust their calendars to yours

- Coordinate with people who want to get on your calendar

- Serve as a double check or reminder

    ◊ Your spouse or staff member might say, "Do you still have that meeting tomorrow with—?)"

    ◊ This might help to avoid double booking or inadvertently omitting a calendar entry

Prioritize which items make it to your calendar—

- Families should agree on which are "golf ball" items and which are not

- Ration the time you spend on commitments that don't directly enhance your job, family, or your health

- If you wish you were somewhere else, or doing something else, consider removing the activity from your calendar

- Just because your spouse says "OK", doesn't mean you should commit to an activity that will take away from your family time in a major way.

Activity Choices

Stick with activities that make you physically and/or emotionally healthy—

- For example, the one hour you worked out at the gym enhanced your physical and emotional health. Sometimes, even more time with friends, or with another activity is just what you need to help with emotional health, but as always, you need to weigh the benefits of that extra time, with the lost time with your family, other activities, or your sleep bank.

- Regardless of the time commitment, watch your excesses

  ◊ The extra drink rarely makes you healthier, or more capable

  ◊ If activities of the night before, hamper your performance the next day, they were probably not good for your long-term health.

Combine activities into the same time slot—

- Activities such as sports, travel, camping, cooking, reading, and table, or video games provide physical and emotional benefits while also enjoying time with friends and family

- Many leaders gain hourglass time by "combining business with pleasure"

  ◊ Having a team meeting over lunch, a glass of wine, or even a round of golf can accomplish work goals while also raising morale

  ◊ Team barbecues or even holiday parties can also be beneficial for building bridges

Note: This table includes strategies to manage time and stress. By focusing on "golf ball" items rather than sand, you will be able to make time for what matters.

How the Leadership Filter Reduces Stress

The leadership filter is a tool to decide what information needs to be passed on to the team and acted upon immediately, what information is best relayed to the team at a later time, and what information doesn't need to be passed on at any time. For example, I often receive information from many sources. My leadership filter, a blend of my brain, heart, job expertise, and other lifetime experiences, helps me make sense of the input and decide what information will make it through the filter and what the timing will be. Relieving my team or family of burdens and stresses that don't apply to them, allows them to move ahead unencumbered by unnecessary negative emotions. My rule is that only items that my team or family needs to know for some positive outcome make it through my filter. As importantly, this filtering process can also relieve my own stress since I spend less energy and time processing responses and emotions of others.

Timely communication of relevant and useful information will always remain a key skill in leadership. Leaders build trust and credibility when they share necessary information with their teams in a timely manner. A special level of respect is often afforded the leader who has the courage and skill to share negative information that is important to a teammate or to the whole team. I suggest those new to leadership find an experienced mentor to serve as a sounding board, especially for sensitive communication challenges.

On the other side of the coin, sharing unnecessary, irrelevant, and negative information, such as gossip, can increase the stress level of the team members and the leader. Team members may respond emotionally to information, even when it is not relevant to them personally or to their job. When a leader vents or shares an account of a difficult conversation or incident that has no present or future relevance, the team might still become stressed by what they hear. The unnecessary information can become amplified and spread, sapping up time and energy. In addition to the energy and productivity lost while the team is emoting over the information, the leader will need to spend stressful hours addressing the unnecessary impact with the team. This is why a leader must use the leadership filter to decide which information is timely and useful to the team and which information is not. Table 3.2 gives specific examples and reasons of what should, and should not pass through the leadership filter and Figure 3.2 illustrates how information processes through the leadership filter.

Table 3.2
Leadership Filter Questions

Leaders should ask themselves the following questions when determining which information to share with their team. Always remember that because you are a leader, your words have more impact than a non-leader's words. The management of your leadership filter will serve as an example and a standard for your teammates.

Questions

1. Is the information you received gossip?

    ◊ If so, don't share it with anybody, on or off the job. Your words count, so does your credibility. The juicier the gossip, the more time spent dealing with the fallout.

2. Is it a complaint?

    ◊ If it doesn't involve your team, don't share it. It has the same negative outcomes as gossip.

3. Does it involve a personnel issue such as the evaluation process or staff discipline?

    ◊ Don't share it. People who are involved with the incident will already know. If you share confidential personnel information, you could be guilty of violating the Federal Right to Privacy Act (FERPA) and the consequences are stiff.

4. Does it involve a student discipline, student counseling, or records issue?

◊ Don't share it. If the person you shared it with repeats their version to someone else, it's you who is subject to FERPA consequences.

5. Does it involve any student health records?

◊ Health records cannot be shared outside immediately involved health professionals without a parental Health Insurance Portability and Accountability Act (HIPAA) release.

6. Does it involve information about any type of child custody issue or question?

◊ Such custody information can't be shared without the written approval of the court documents.

7. Is the information important for a teammate to be able to do their job better?

◊ If you think it is, decide who on the team needs to know. If the whole team can benefit, meet with the whole team together so they all hear the information the same way, at the same time, and have time to have a clarifying conversation. Don't leak it out sporadically. If a teammate is not present, it's a priority to let them know about the information as early as possible

8. Does this information need to be passed on to my team immediately?

◊ This is for a safety issue, a schedule change, or a news item that everyone needs to know about.

◊ It is important to put major news items in writing when you make any such announcements.

◊ Social media has proven to be an effective way to get important information out to large groups.

◊ REMEMBER, you are the leader and you will choose the words that are in the message.

■ Some people put a negative connotation on the word "spin" at times like this, but I always use the hammer analogy and select words that are the least damaging or traumatizing, while still getting the whole message out. I call that a positive and honest spin. No exaggerating. No hyperbole.

Actions

1. Decide which teammates need to get the information and when do they need it—

    ◊ Team members who will surely be, or may be impacted need to hear your report (with positive, honest vocabulary) asap if the information is urgent. Routine announcements that aren't time sensitive can be included in weekly newsletters, or announcements—

       ■ I err on the side of informing any teammate that has an even remote chance of ever needing the information.

       ■ If tonight's event is canceled, moved to another location, or had it's time changed, of course, let them know immediately.

       ■ If the change is weeks or more away, you can include it with your weekly information so it doesn't get lost in the shuffle.

Note: This table shares questions and tips to ask yourself as you use your leadership filter.

Figure 3.2
Leadership Filter Diagram

OUT

How will you spin it? (i.e. half full or half empty?)

Who needs to know?

leadership filter
YOU
1. Brain
2. Heart
3. Experience
4. Instincts
5. Goals

Complaints

Gossip

Suggestions

Concerns

Heads-up

IN

Note: This diagram illustrates how the leadership filter operates by taking in information and then making a decision about how to process it, and eventually how and to whom to communicate it.

The Hourglass and Leadership Filter Work Together

Working in synergy, my hourglass and leadership filter help me manage stress in my personal and professional life. These two strategies connect through their strong similarities of purpose, impact, and simplicity. They are both tightly connected to the two major factors that cause work stress— too little time and/or too much to accomplish. On many occasions over the years, I recall thinking— "If I only had more time to work on this or that task on my to-do list, I could complete them with little, or no stress." These tasks were often routine and in areas where I had the skills to easily complete them. Some were even enjoyable, important, and rewarding. If I could only have a few more hours each day, I could complete them and not be stressed at all. The other side of this dichotomy is that with a reasonable number of tasks, I could probably enjoy my work and complete my tasks with little or no stress. In the following paragraphs and in Table 3.2, I share detailed, realistic ways to reduce your stress, by more effectively managing your time and by removing a major factor in your workload.

Over the years, many positive outcomes have resulted from using my leadership filter effectively. Remember— a key ingredient in everyone's filter is their own life experience and expertise. As my experience and expertise have grown, I have been able to use my filter in more precise ways. Personal experience, including plenty of hard knocks, taught me important lessons about who really needs to know what. My improved use of the leadership filter simplified many team relationships and allowed me to address challenges and delegate my team more accurately. Finally, on several specific occasions in my various positions, office staff members and building level leaders have said such things as, "Thank you for just letting us work." and "Thank you for not wrapping us up in all of the negative stuff you have to deal with." These responses showed me that avoiding sharing every detail of my job benefitted my faculty, staff, and colleagues in measurable ways.

How Does Not Majoring in the Minors Work?

To illustrate how to avoid *Majoring in the Minors,* I've selected four examples that illustrate how to not overreact and allow yourself to be derailed. Two of the examples are personal ones from my time teaching Senior Boys English and from working in my administrator role. The other two examples are from professional sports and serve to illustrate how this strategy works in real-world situations.

Senior Boys Teach Their Teacher About Majoring in the Minors

Each year, Senior Boys English grew into a family environment, and as the year progressed, a sense of hope grew. A "good gang" mentality emerged causing trust and a feeling of safety. Most of the young men in Senior Boys English had been in school together since kindergarten, and they knew intimately of each other's life stories. One year, I taught Chad, and the first time he had a grand mal epileptic seizure in class, I got physically dizzy with panic. But, the guys remained calm. They moved the chairs away, formed a large circle, and physically supported him. They kept Chad on his feet, holding him under his arms as they passed him around the room. Jared, known as the toughest and rowdiest kid in the school, was the clear leader. When Chad's seizure subsided, it was Jared who grabbed a towel from the back of the room and gently wiped Chad's face and clothes.

My pre-med education and teaching methods courses had not prepared me for that moment. Chad's seizure was a major event to me, and I became derailed emotionally and physically. I had never witnessed a grand mal seizure. I was shaken, and though I tried to act composed, the guys could tell I was panicked. They pretty much ignored me as they put the chairs back in rows and got ready to get back to work. Chad was back in his seat with a smile, as if to say, "What are you waiting for, Mr. Amend? Let's get to work." On the other hand, many of these guys had guided Chad through his epileptic seizures for twelve years. This was a common experience for them, so it was not a major deal. They didn't become derailed.

Chad had five more seizures in our class that year. I eventually joined the circle and grew in confidence that I didn't need to overreact and be derailed by Chad's seizures. One life lesson Chad and the guys taught me was that one person's major event may be another person's minor event. They also showed me that with mentoring, patience, and love, my major could evolve into a minor.

Fighting or Scuffling:
How Do You Want to Spend the Rest of Your Day?

Nick was a mountain of a man and was one of the kindest, most sensitive, caring people I ever worked with. He loved kids, and the students and parents loved him back. Nick taught and coached at the middle school in my district for many years before I started working there. He was a legend for all the right reasons. As superintendent, I promoted Nick to middle school principal.

During his second week on his new job, he came into my office with two 8th grade boys in tow. He seated the kids in the waiting area with the secretary, came into my office, and closed the door. His face was red, and he was fired up with frustration. In a soft, slow voice, I said, "Sit down here, Nick," and pointed to the chair in my office. "What's going on, man? Talk to me." He told me, "Well, I was just checking the boy's locker room after PE, and these two young men were wrestling on the cement floor."

Nick knew we had a firm rule that defined fighting, and the penalty for fighting was out of school suspensions for three days. Though this was his first discipline incident as principal at the school, Nick knew the suspension process included separate meetings with both sets of parents and then sending the students home. He explained these high energy kids were good student athletes and leaders in the school. Nick didn't want to suspend the boys— he didn't want to make a major incident out of a minor incident.

Because the boys were wrestling on the floor when he walked into the locker room, and both had insisted that neither had struck each other, I told Nick that he could call it scuffling rather than fighting. With a slight smile, Nick said, "That sounds good to me, Boss." I said, "Then go back out there and take the kids back to your office. Put your hands on their shoulders, look them straight in the eye nice and close, and say, 'You both know you shouldn't have been scuffling in that locker room. Somebody could have gotten hurt. Now, if you keep your nose clean for the rest of the year, I won't need to call your folks about this.'" Both young men breathed a huge sigh of relief and went on to have a squeaky clean 8th grade year, remaining strong, positive leaders in their class.

As we worked together over the next eight years, Nick became a master at deciding whether an issue was major or minor. His positive instincts allowed him to continue building strong trust bridges with the kids, staff, and community. When the issue was major, he tackled it head on until it was resolved. Nick's reputation for knowing what to hear and what not to hear, and for not majoring in the minors built and maintained trust bridges that allowed him to retain his credibility during tough, major issues.

Knowing What to See and What Not to See

A common example of not majoring in the minors is found with experienced sports officials. Professional sports officials have long said that on virtually every play in the game, some penalty could be called, thus interrupting the flow of the game. In football, these plays often happen at the line of scrimmage, where the biggest and strongest players on the field are battling for an advantage. Football's rules in the areas of offensive and defensive holding are complex and split-second decisions need to be made. If the infraction impacted the play, a flag is thrown, the game stops, and the penalty assessed. Likewise, basketball officials say if they went by the letter of the law in the rule book and called all of the jostling in the post, the hand checking, the ball handling, and the traveling, they would never finish a ball game. Officials who make unnecessary calls are not respected and usually are not assigned to big games for that reason. In post-game interviews, experienced coaches will often say "After we adjusted to how much physical contact these officials allowed without calling a penalty or foul, we were fine."

Adjusting to What the Leader Views as Major or Minor

The concept of adjusting to what is major or minor in the eyes of the leader is also a key factor in how smoothly a business team or family functions. The two key factors that impact how quickly and accurately a team or family can learn what is major and minor are consistency and predictability. Inconsistent leaders are not predictable. They can derail their team with their random or indecisive decision making. Their teams are forced to work in a world of guessing and trial/error, causing team members to become tentative in their decision-making due to fear of having to retrace their steps if they didn't guess right. On the other hand, a team or family working with a leader that is predictable can proceed with confidence, based on their accurate understanding of what their leader views as major or minor.

In the area of team or individual discipline, the leader may want to adjust their normal major-minor standards in order to "send a message" or "spruce up" their team's performance in some area. This change is often a procedural or behavioral expectation the leader thinks will make the team more successful. The leader needs to be clear and honest with their team about the change. The leader also needs to make sure that they're not violating the 95% rule with their decision (see Chapter 4 for more on "The 95% Rule"). If the leader overreacts or places blame on the wrong people, the team may suffer the negative consequences of violating the 95% rule, including the weakening of trust bridges.

Conclusion

In this chapter, readers learned about hourglass and leadership filter strategies. The hourglass clarifies priorities in life and provides guidance to deciding which deserve the focus of our time and effort. The specific strategies offered in the leadership filter section can reduce stress both on and off the job. When the hourglass and leadership filter strategies are combined, productivity can increase, and stress level can be dramatically reduced. The real-world examples of how to avoid majoring in the minors apply in any business or family environment. Whether in a classroom, a one-on-one situation, a family setting, or a team environment, the leader's ability to be both consistent and predictable will be key factors in how quickly and how well people will be able to respond positively to their leadership.

Use Table 3.3 to create your action plan for using the strategies in this chapter. You will want to focus on how to prioritize your time and activities, as well as how to use your own leadership filter more effectively.

Table 3.3
Action Plan: Don't Major in the Minors

What are two takeaways from this section? 1. 2.
What two strategies will you use to improve your prioritizing skills? 1. 2.
What steps will you take now? (Action Step for Don't Major in the Minors)

Note: This table provides readers with a place to apply what they have learned about prioritizing in every part of their life. The use of the hourglass analogy and your personal leadership filter can become important stress reducers in any area of your life.

CHAPTER 4

TOOL #4: THE 95% RULE

The 95% Rule states, "A leader will not punish the majority of their team, in order to address the undesired behavior of a minority of their team."

This chapter begins by examining common 95% rule dynamics. Any expectation that is violated in your professional or personal life could apply to the 95% rule if there is a group of people involved. Readers should also be aware that 95% is used as a percentage to illustrate that the majority should not be punished for the actions of the minority, and actual percentages might not align to 95% (i.e. 66% vs. 33%, 75% vs. 25%; any percentage that displays the majority/minority works). It could be as simple as a decision between children and parents— one child breaks a rule, so the parents change the rule for all the kids in the home.

The chapter goes on to discuss consequences that arise from violating or respecting the 95% rule. There are impacts when penalizing everyone for the behavior of a few. The majority, the 95%, is impacted, and a 95% rule violation also impacts the 5%. This group is small in number but capable of creating serious negative impacts on the leader's effectiveness and the team's performance. The potential positive and negative impacts on the leader by choosing either to honor or break the 95% rule will also be considered. Some stories shared in this chapter address how teams pick up the pieces after a leader has violated the 95% rule. These teams focus on how to create positive, healing, and bridge-building outcomes out of a tough situation rather than allowing a negative outcome to prevail for their team.

Leading Through the Difficult Dynamics of a 95% Situation

Confronting negative behavior in team members is one of the toughest parts of a leader's job. That's why many people would rather spend 40 hours doing hard, physical labor in harsh conditions than spend 40 minutes behind closed doors in a tough one-on-one conversation. Given a choice, many people choose not to engage in tough, emotional conversations. However, convening and succeeding in tough conversations separates great leaders from lesser leaders. Having the courage and ability to confront the negative behavior will make the team stronger and build credibility for the leader. Stopping negative behavior is a survival skill for high performing teams and ensures long-term success for a leader. By using SIDWI skills and other strategies in this book, leaders will improve their ability to address negative issues during one-on-one conversations (see Chapter 1 for more details about SIDWI). Tough conversations become easier as the leader's skills, confidence and credibility grow.

Understanding the human dynamics around the 95% rule, reinforces the reality that all employees will not be treated the same way in every situation. Team members in the 95% group who have embraced the team's goals and are trying to be strong team players receive support and affirmation. The 5% who either overtly or covertly act against the leader and/or the team goals receive swift action to address their behavior. The team is watching, and credibility is at stake with both groups when a response is delayed. In this important credibility test, leaders must summon the courage to face hard conversations directly. The stakes are high for everybody, and until the 5% group is dealt with directly, negative people will continue to be barriers to the team's ability to reach goals, and to the leader's credibility and effectiveness.

95% Rule Factors

In the following section, the dynamics of the 95% rule are shared, including the various ways the 95% rule can impact the team and the leader. By sharing a specific example to illustrate the 95% rule in action, readers will visualize the key concepts in this chapter— protecting the innocent from being treated like the guilty, having the skills and courage to deal firmly with offenders, and picking up the pieces and turning them into wins in real-life situations.

Factor 1: Violating the 95% rule. The principal enters the faculty meeting with body language that shows he's very upset. It immediately becomes clear that some faculty have not been adhering to expectations that had been included in team policies and procedures. The leader addresses the entire staff; however, 95% of the team has been following the policies. Only 5% of the people are in violation, yet the leader admonishes everybody in the room. What's wrong with this picture?

There are different reasons why a leader might violate the 95% rule. One of the most common reasons is that the leader doesn't feel confident or competent enough to confront the violators one-on-one. One-on-one conversation about difficult topics, with difficult people is one of the toughest duties any leader must face (see Chapter 1: SIDWI for strategies to conduct these difficult conversations). Another reason is the leader might mistakenly think it will be quicker and easier to reprimand the whole team rather than just dealing with the small group of offenders. A third reason, which would probably go unstated, is in seeking to avoid further violations going forward, the leader might think the innocent teammates can also benefit from his message. The leader mistakenly thought the innocent team members didn't mind, or were not offended. In short, the leader misjudged how the public reprimand produced negative outcomes from the 95% group who had been following the rules all along.

Factor 2: Impact on the innocent 95%. In order to illustrate how the innocent 95% are impacted when the 95% rule is violated, I share a personal experience that occurred early in my teaching career.

At 7:05 AM, I sat in the band room with the entire faculty (125 colleagues) as we waited for the weekly 7:00 AM staff meeting to start. The door swung open, and I noticed the principal's body language as he charged into the room. His red, angry face alerted us all that there was a potential problem. He started to speak in a pitched voice. Our boss had four items that he wanted to address: (1) arriving late, (2) leaving early, (3) using the back parking lot to avoid getting caught leaving early or arriving late, and (4) not bothering to write comments on the progress reports that had gone home with students the previous Friday. After addressing those four items, he briefly covered three other non-related agenda items, and the meeting was over. There was no time for questions, input, or response. As he walked out through the double doors, the band room was silent. Finally, I got up and walked toward my classroom. As an innocent team member, I was disappointed, wounded, and angry. I resented receiving a public reprimand for actions I was completely innocent of doing. As one of the 95%, I took pride in my efforts, integrity, and professionalism, and the public reprimand insulted me and my innocent teammates.

My experience illustrates that the innocent 95% experience frustration and resentment when they are included in a reprimand they do not deserve. Because the principal in this example took out his anger on all 125 faculty members rather than the 5-10 faculty that actually had failed to meet expectations, he lost respect from all faculty. Innocent faculty entered their classrooms that day already upset, their day off to a bad start, due to failure by their leader to obey the 95% rule.

Factor 3: Impact on the 5%. In addition to the negative impacts felt by the 95%, the faculty meeting described above did not work to change the behavior of the 5%. One major failure was the 5% rule violators were never identified or held accountable in any way. Whoever they were, they walked out of the meeting without any consequences for their actions. The 5% group may have left the meeting thinking, "If the boss isn't going to confront us when we don't follow the rules, why should we change our approach?" Because the boss did not confront the behavior of this small non-compliant group, and because he included innocent team members in his comments, he ended up losing credibility, trust and respect with both groups.

As leaders, parents, and coaches, we must be aware that violating the 95% rule does not change the behavior of the 5%. Only by directly addressing the 5% in one-on-one meetings with each violator, will the leader be able to produce a positive change in behavior. By singling out the violators of a rule or expectation, and being brave enough to confront the undesired behavior, the leader is demonstrating true leadership skills. The leader can maintain the violators' dignity by practicing SIDWI skills (Chapter 1). Taking time to listen and learn can lead to trust bridges between the leader and team member. The leader may also learn there might have been a good reason the staff member didn't meet the expectation.

In addition to using SIDWI strategies, the leader can apply the leadership filter (see Chapter 3) to this situation, ultimately deciding that the majority of the team doesn't need to know the specifics around the rule violations or the one-on-one conversations. Filtering out details allows team members to continue working without added stress and distraction. In addition to these stress relieving outcomes, handling the process with appropriate confidentiality builds stronger trust between the leader and the entire team.

Factor 4: Impact on the boss. Credibility is the currency of leadership, and the goal is to build trust bridges between ourselves and our teams. When the leader follows the 95% rule, it positively impacts the trust bridges being built throughout the team. However, violating the 95% rule creates a set of sensitive and timely challenges for the leader. Violating the 95% rule means using a sledgehammer approach with the entire faculty when, in reality, the sledgehammer may not even need to be taken out of the pickup truck (see Chapter 2). When the 95% rule is violated, the leader's trust bridge between all team members is damaged.

In the staff meeting example, the boss broke the popsicle sticks, and Elmer's trust glue will need to be added to repair the relationships between the leader and all of the team members. Because the comments were made to a large group of people, the 95% group took the comments personally. Regardless of why the boss made his decision, I wondered if I would be treated with respect in the future after that faculty meeting so many years ago. Trust bridges had been violated in a public and personal way. Previous feelings of safety, security. and confidence had been severely compromised. The 95% group wondered, "Is this the way we're going to be doing business around here?" On the other hand, the leader's credibility with the rule violators (the 5%) also suffered. The 5% witnessed the leader taking out frustration on the entire team when just a few people had broken the rule. The 5% knew who they were, and because the leader didn't confront them directly, their relationship—which could have been strengthened with a SIDWI conversation—suffered instead.

Factor 5: Picking up the pieces. Leaders may realize they reacted emotionally and inappropriately to a situation. This may happen immediately afterward, coming through feedback from team members who feel upset, or much later—after introspection by the leader or after behavior doesn't change (or worsens). Either way, the leader will need to begin repairing the relationship with the team (the 95% and the 5%). This section offers some strategies for rebuilding and repairing trust bridges that have been damaged after a 95% violation. If the leader realizes the error immediately after the meeting, a written apology to the faculty can begin to repair the bridge between all parties. I suggest the apology be written and distributed as soon as the leader realizes the error.

In the example from the faculty meeting described above, a written apology could have helped. The principal could have sent a note out to faculty, for example. The apology should be written to both the 95% and the 5% groups. Possible wording for the apology are included in Table 4.1. This note should be written in a personal voice, demonstrating to the faculty who receive it that the leader truly cares about the mistake and wants to fix it. The leader allows the team to see vulnerability by admitting the error and shows willingness to grow by planning for moving forward.

Table 4.1
Sample Apology Letter 1

Dear Faculty,

   This note is to apologize for how I handled [this morning's] *staff meeting. I was wrong to group the whole team together when my comments needed to be directed to a small number of team members. In the future, I will address such concerns with only the individuals who need to hear my message. If you want to speak to me about* [today's meeting], *let me know, and we'll set up a time to meet. Again, I apologize for my mistake and look forward to moving ahead as a united team.*

Respectfully,
[Harry]

Note: Parts of the letter that should be adjusted and personalized are in brackets.

In cases where the mistake is only realized much later after the situation, leaders must take different steps to repair the relationship with the team in hopes of rebuilding any damaged relationships moving into the future. The first step is to research the original situation. The second step is to send a letter similar to the sample above, but including a clear statement that after becoming aware of details about this issue, you realize an apology is in order. Possible wording for this letter is included in Table 4.2.

Table 4.2
Sample Apology Letter 2

Dear Faculty,

This letter is to bring you up to date on information that was shared at our [January 3rd] *meeting, and my response to the whole staff at that time.*

At that meeting [a staff member shared a frustration about procedures that were being violated regarding use of the copy machine]. *At that time, I thought the concern was about the whole staff, and I directed my corrective statement as if every staff member needed to hear it. I have since learned that the issue was with only a couple staff members. First, I want to apologize for assuming you were all involved, and for including innocent team members in my corrective comments. Second, I want the whole staff to know that I* [will be meeting] *one-on-one with each of the people who were involved in the issue. Though I won't be sharing any of the details from our conversations, I am confident that the conversations will be productive. In the future, I will be sure to do the necessary research to determine what my response should be on an issue before responding publicly or privately with staff members.*

The procedures that we have for [using the copy room] *are set up to benefit us all, so I trust we will all use those procedures in the future. I've attached a current copy of the procedures to this letter for your reference.* [I understand that we haven't updated these procedures since we got our new copying equipment and lease agreement, so if you want to volunteer to be on a committee to update our procedures, please let me know. We'll start meeting after Spring Vacation, and volunteers will be compensated at the District Committee pay rate.]

As always, if you want to visit in private about this letter, please let me know and we'll set up a time to meet.

Sincerely,
[Harry]

Note: Parts of the letter that should be adjusted and personalized are in brackets.

This letter does several things: (1) it explains why the leader first chose to address the issue publicly, (2) it acknowledges that doing so was a mistake, (3) it apologizes to the innocent staff members who received corrective comments in error, (4) it lets the entire faculty know that the 5% people were/will be held accountable through one-on-one meetings with the leader, and (5) it assures the entire staff that the leader will research and think before taking action in the future. Each of these actions ensure the staff that the leader has taken positive steps moving forward. The letter also offers the 95% a chance to work on a committee to address the issue and make possible changes to the current policy if necessary.

Each of the letters above could work to repair damaged relationships caused by 95% rule violations. Sending a letter to the team shows that the leader is addressing the issue personally and wants to take the time to ensure that all of the team members are aware of the solutions. Offering for team members to review and revise the current rule or procedure involves the team in finding a solution that will work for all—and moves the entire team into the grey area of problem solving. The solutions each type of situation focuses on can result in repairing the trust bridges and improving the work environment for the whole team.

Factor 6: Steps for successful conversations with the 5% group. In the following section, I have included recommendations that will facilitate the tough conversations that must be had with the 5%. I conduct individual meetings with the 5% using SIDWI skills (listen, learn, and lead), planning to use three hammer sizes. Because I have learned that a team member may be part of the majority in one situation, but be in the 5% in another situation, I don't hesitate to include suggestions for both praise and corrections in the same conversation and the hammer strategies are effective for facilitating this type of nuance. In the sections that follow, specific strategies for successful conversations with the 5% align with these strategies (For more information about hammer strategies, see Chapter 2).

Start with small hammer strategies. I start with a smaller hammer approach, which allows me to be patient, positive, and ready to handle the high emotions. As a reminder, small hammer approaches consider the fragile emotions of team members and attempt to solve conflicts without damaging the trust bridge.

I start the meeting letting the team member know why the meeting has been called (i.e. rule violation), and then begin using the first step of SIDWI, "Listen." I allow them to talk first and take as much time as they need. They explain why they broke the rule or expectation. Their non-verbal language allows me to gain additional insight. I write down their exact words. After they finish, I suggest a ten-minute break and use that time to highlight areas of their statement that I can use to move them into the grey area.

Moving into the grey area: Middle-sized hammer strategies. When they come back into the room, I use mid-sized hammer strategies as we prepare to move into the grey area, working to strengthen the fragile trust bridge we are trying to build. The second step of SIDWI, "Learn," helps me to figure out possible solutions. My goal is to find a positive, lasting result. By moving into the grey area, they begin to feel some power, even though, in fact, I am the one in power. I keep my body language neutral, including no smiling—as suggested in the hammer strategy section (see Chapter 2). There is no friendly small talk that might lessen their focus or the strong interpretation of the message they are receiving.

Though I may not be convinced by the excuses they give, I don't interrupt. I make notes of possible solutions and ideas as they speak, and I interrupt occasionally to ask clarifying questions. Their reasons for violating the rule or expectation may include not remembering some of the expectations, thinking some of the rules are only guidelines, or not agreeing with a new approach because they liked the old way better. Finally, they may also confide that their previous leader let them make their own decisions, did not meet with them one-on-one to confront any non-compliant behavior, or didn't follow-up when they didn't comply with rules or expectations. During this meeting, I do not challenge their intent or truthfulness. I accept their words and make sure to respond only to the current issue, not expanding the conversation to include any other issues or behavior.

Finishing with a heavy hammer approach. Using a heavy hammer (sledgehammer) approach, I finally confront their behavior in a direct and unambiguous way, "Leading" (step 3 of SIDWI) to a solution.

I make sure to express my expectations and requirements in black and white terms. This part of the meeting reminds the person what they did to end up in this conversation and that they are accountable for their behavior. Though I may not be convinced by the excuses they gave for their non-compliant behaviors, my message is clear, and I'm ready to move ahead and see how things go with them in the future. After going over all of my ideas, I end by stating clearly,

"I believe that these [changes, expectations, rules, etc.] are in the best interest of our team and I expect everyone on the team to comply with them. If you disagree, or have questions about any area in the future, I'm telling you, now, to come to me for clarification. Do you have any questions about anything we've covered today?"

After they ask any questions, I stand up, look the person in the eye, and shake their hand as they leave the room. Their new behavior expectations are now crystal clear as they leave the room. Because I know I will have similar conversations with other team members in the future, and I want to be consistent, I close my door and complete my notes, being sure to fill in key, exact quotes I remember from the meeting, noting pieces that worked well or didn't work as well so I can continue to improve my leadership skills moving forward.

As I did with SIDWI in Chapter 1, I've taken extra time in this chapter to provide the detail necessary to succeed in important, difficult, and emotional conversations with non-compliant teammates. Despite their difficulty,

I encourage you to have these conversations with difficult team members, and I remind you that, "The gain will be worth the pain" in these difficult conversations.

Using the 95% Rule to Lead your Team to Success

I've included two stories to illustrate the 95% rule. "What Could She be Thinking?" describes a new leader who lacked information and made a hair-trigger decision during her second staff meeting. One impact was a loss of credibility among many members of her 125-person team. However, her quick response to the mistake taught her (and can teach us) an important lesson about restoring credibility with a team. "Do I Need to get a 2 x 4?" illustrates a strong leader who has the wisdom and courage to have a private one-on-one conversation to confront and change the behavior of a valued teammate.

What Could She Be Thinking?

Though this incident happened early in my teaching career, it is still clear in my mind today. Our 125 staff members were gathered in the band room for a morning meeting and I was in my usual seat in the top back row. When the new principal reached the "New Business" part of the agenda, a diminutive science teacher stood up and in an emotional voice stated,

"Last night about 5:00 PM, I almost got run over by a boy running in the halls. I was coming out of my classroom, and this boy ran by. I would have been run over if he hadn't dodged me. If he had hit me, I know I would have been seriously injured. So, I think we need to make a rule that there should be no running in our halls."

This proposal was problematic. The floor plan of the school was a large, open rectangle lined with classrooms on both sides, and the halls were a perfect running track. For over 22 years, the rectangular hall space had been used as an inside track for PE classes, sports teams, and even staff members who needed a place to run during time when inclement weather made running outside impossible. Runners were coached to run with caution, and there had been no previous reports of near-death experiences in over 22 years. If the science teacher's new "rule" was put into policy, PE classes, athletes, coaches, and staff members no longer had a space to run during the long winter months.

After the science teacher sat down, without thought or consideration of the impact her decision would have on the entire school community, the principal simply decreed a new rule that made running in the hallways illegal. The staff was in shock. The emotional response was immediate. Though some felt sorry for her, others lost confidence as her voice cracked and her body language revealed her high level of anxiety. By the end of the day, the principal rescinded her decision, along with an apology. She had allowed one staff member to impact 95% of her colleagues in a negative way. Because the principal openly took responsibility for her hair-trigger decision, she turned what started as a negative incident to many staff members into an opportunity to build credibility with her new team.

The new principal learned a major leadership lesson that day— to not make decisions without considering all sides of an issue. Before announcing a decision, she should have given herself time to learn the facts and politics surrounding the situation. Looking back, if the principal had not been new to the job, she would have known this particular science teacher was part of the 5% who were not supportive of the sports teams or PE activities. She may also have considered how a decision about the inside "track" impacted the rest of the school community (the 95%). To give herself time to learn about all sides of the issue, she could have said, "I haven't been aware of this issue. Let me take some time to put my thoughts together. I'll get back to everybody." She could have chosen a different way to handle the complaint by saying, "Let's not have any running until I get back to you," or "Coaches, please remind your athletes to watch out for other people in the halls while they're running." These responses would make sense to most of the staff and would have been respected by both points of view. After giving herself time to research the issue and make a decision, she could have met with the science teacher to explain her decision. Then she could have announced her decision and openly thanked people on both sides of the issue for caring enough to step forward and be heard.

Do I Have to Hit You in the Head With a 2 x 4?

The following example involves one of my closest friends, Marty. I started working for Marty when I became the principal of a 300-student high school. He was the superintendent of the district, but I had known him for over 17 years, both personally and professionally. We shared a love of kids and baseball, and I had even signed two of his sons to professional baseball contracts in my role as a part-time baseball scout. Our trust bridge was strong—built over many common experiences in and out of education. Over the years, I learned some important things from Marty that relate directly to *The Ten Tools*, including SIDWI, leave the sledgehammer in the pick-up truck, and the 95% rule.

Marty understood the strength of trust bridges, which defined his ability to lead his team. Marty was a straight shooter who stood his ground in any conversation. On many occasions throughout the years, I saw tempers flare and people leave a setting frustrated and angry with Marty. But people knew Marty was a bridge-builder, and even when they adamantly disagreed with him, people trusted Marty. Especially during these most trying circumstances, Marty followed up with the people, and kept his trust bridges strong. His sincerity, trust, and concern for the other person created strong glue, and he knew how to use it to repair, rebuild, and reinforce a bridge. Marty worked hard to build trust bridges with his team, and even when faced with challenging situations, Marty prioritized building those bridges.

The softball field fiasco. I learned about the 95% rule from Marty firsthand. The example that follows happened during my first year as high school principal.

In the fall, Marty and I had walked down to check out the lower softball field. I wanted to get his permission to bring in a load of dirt to improve the field. It was a small field, with 60 foot distance between the bases, and I knew a load of dirt would improve the quality and the safety of the field. Marty approved the purchase order for the load, which needed to wait until spring when the ground dried enough for the dump truck to get in and out safely. The weather cooperated and during spring vacation, I called a contractor to bring in the load of dirt. I met the truck driver with the small district tractor to guide him down to the field.

As luck had it, the driver turned out to be one of my former baseball players. He now worked with his dad in the dirt business. I gave him the purchase order, signed for the delivery, and headed for the tractor, excited to spread the new dirt and drag the field. Before climbing back into the truck, he said, "Hey, Coach, I just talked to my dad, and he wants to know if you'd like another load of dirt. On the house." I couldn't resist.

The second load came in a much bigger truck, and unlike the first load, this was the highest quality dirt, free of pebbles and clumps—like they used at pro ballparks. Three hours later, I finished dragging the field, and it was beautiful. The newly manicured dirt field with 90 foot bases was perfect for either softball or baseball. At the time, my adrenaline was running high; I had created this new baseball field where a bumpy, rutted little softball field had existed just hours before. I remember wishing for a camera to record this amazing improvement. I was not thinking about calling Marty to get permission for the extra dirt and the larger field. Even though I had several days between when I worked on the field and when he returned to the district, I thought Marty would be happy about the improvement, so I didn't consider needing to ask him or let him know.

But, I quickly discovered my mistake. Because I made a decision to make a permanent, visible change to school property without his permission, I was part of the 5% group that needed to be dealt with firmly by the boss. When Marty walked into my office that Monday morning his face was beet red. Marty started off the conversation with a sledgehammer to get my attention. He slammed my office door and sputtered, "What the _ _ _ _ did you do down there?" I started to talk and he interrupted, "I told you, you could put a load of dirt on the softball field and you made a baseball field out of it. Do I have to hit you in the forehead with a 2 x 4?" He continued, "What made you think you could do that without my permission? Do you think you're running this district?" I sat there in stunned silence, my eyes tearing up. I sensed that bringing in the extra dirt and expanding the field was not the biggest problem here. With our close friendship, it hadn't occurred to me that the extra dirt would be a problem with Marty—and the dirt wasn't—not really. Marty was both angry and disappointed. I was wrong to not keep him informed about the expanded field. Marty didn't want to damage our strong trust bridge, but he did want to get his clear message across— he was my boss, and I needed to respect him enough to get his permission and keep him in the loop on decisions that had to do with the school district.

The lessons I learned from Marty that day helped me many times over the years. I needed to hold the teammate accountable. I've had to use a sledge-hammer with team members—even when they were my friends and close colleagues. Marty's decision to treat me with the small hammer strategies of reconciliation and trust at the end of our emotional one-on-one conversation, taught me the importance of maintaining and strengthening a trust bridge, especially after a difficult conversation. Finally, as a first year principal still trying to earn credibility, I appreciated that Marty confronted me one-on-one with the door closed. I also appreciated, and learned an important lesson, when Marty didn't share our issue with other staff members in the district. Because of how he respected me that day, I learned how to protect a team member's dignity and credibility—both during and after a tough meeting. Marty didn't want to devastate me, but he did want to change my behavior. Marty's actions during my 5% situation became a model for me when dealing with tough conversations over the years.

Conclusion

In this chapter, readers learned that obeying or breaking the 95% rule makes a difference in the leader's credibility and the relationship with the team. We began the chapter by exploring the dynamics of the 95% rule, including six important factors that leaders need to know. Several reasons for obeying the 95% rule were shared, and we learned that when the 95% rule is not followed, everyone on the team is impacted. Leaders need to remember that they lose credibility every time they fail to confront negative behavior and we found that when the 5% people aren't confronted directly about broken rules or bad behavior, they can become even bolder, continuing negative behaviors without fear.

Throughout the chapter, readers have made connections between the 95% rule and the previous tools (specifically, SIDWI and leave the sledge-hammer in the pick-up truck). The chapter concluded with the stories of a new leader who learned how to practice the 95% rule and a veteran leader who built strong trust bridges, while at the same time confronting a 5% issue with a team member. Through practice and learning from our mistakes, we all can learn to follow the 95% rule in our home, work, and personal lives. Complete the action plan that follows to plan to ways to use these strategies in our own leadership (see Table 4.3).

Table 4.3
Action Plan: The 95% Rule

What are two takeaways from this section?
1.
2.
What two strategies will you use to remember the 95% rule?
1.
2.
What steps will you take now? (Action Step for The 95% Rule)

Note: This table provides readers with a place to apply the 95% rule when leading their families and their teams. Success in confronting and resolving issues with the 5% group will be key to your leadership success.

CHAPTER 5

TOOL #5: DON'T KICK A SLEEPING DOBERMAN

In "Don't Kick a Sleeping Doberman," I use the Doberman Pinscher's temperament to compare team members who respond with Doberman-like behaviors in certain situations. Doberman Pinschers originated in Germany during the late 19th century and were originally bred as guard dogs. Today's Doberman Pinschers are obedient and devoted; easily motivated and trainable; and protective, excellent guard dogs, but they can be aggressive, fearful, or snappy if not socialized properly, and overprotective when startled or cornered. They are classified as working, guardian dogs by both the American Kennel Club and the United Kennel Club. After a school assembly one year, I remember a professional guard dog trainer laughing and telling me, "Never startle or suddenly wake-up a Doberman. The results are never pretty." I have always remembered this, and it became the basis for Tool #5. I share this leadership analogy because it relates to the many decisions a leader makes when creating relationships and maintaining continuity and cohesiveness on a team that contains members that respond in overprotective, fearful, and sometimes aggressive ways. Many lessons throughout this book relate to the Doberman concepts in this chapter.

My direct experiences and observations influenced my decision to select the Doberman breed for this chapter. Doberman Pinschers can be great family dogs; in fact, I have close friends whose Dobermans are docile and sweet with their families because they were socialized and trained properly. I have witnessed the fact that as guard dogs, Dobermans can be very effective at protecting their territory and aggressive to people they don't know or like. Their loyalty and over-protectiveness toward their families is evident. When I enter the home or yard of friends who own these dogs, the dogs know I am a stranger and act fiercely loyal until they know it's okay for me to be there, even barking, growling, and lunging at me when I walk up to the door of the house.

This chapter examines the different types of decisions that any leader may face during a normal work day. The Doberman describes the emotions (similar to Doberman Pinschers reactions in certain situations) resulting from a decision. The person or the decision provokes an aggressive and emotional response that complicates the interaction. The two primary approaches discussed in this chapter are the leader directly intervening, or the leader encouraging the team to address the issue itself. A third, less-used approach available to the leader, is not responding at all to making the decision. This chapter shares reasons, factors, and criteria that help the leader make the decision whether to intervene, let the team handle it, or not respond at all. Pros and cons of each decision making strategy will be discussed in detail.

Analyzing the Potential Dobermans and Stakes in the Decision

Leaders need to make countless decisions in support of their families and teams. These decisions can be divided into two different types: no-brainer decisions and decisions that require careful deliberation, planning, and implementation.

No-Brainer Decisions

In no-brainer decisions, the need to respond or not respond seems obvious. If the issue demands a response, the leader knows they need to develop a strategy to address the issue and then decide whether to intervene personally or let the team address the solution.

High stakes decisions. The first type of decision, the high stakes decision, is a no-brainer because of the facts surrounding the situation, such as urgency or the high stakes of the outcome. The need to act immediately is obvious, and regardless of the cost, either the leader, or the team must kick this sleeping Doberman. In this chapter, rather than repeating the types of situations that require a sledgehammer, which are already described in Chapter 2, the focus is on strategies and the follow-up processes for navigating the emotional outcomes resulting from sledgehammers. Doberman traits such as anger and fierce protectiveness by teammates are key dynamics in the process if the leader uses sledgehammer strategies. The leader and the team will be reminded in advance of the clean-up, both in healing and implementing a new solution, that will occur if the primary hammer size used is the sledgehammer.

Lower stakes decisions. The second type of no-brainer decision happens at the other end of the decision-making spectrum. In these situations, the leader chooses to not confront the Doberman directly at that time. "Letting the Doberman sleep" rather than dealing with the emotional and stressful reaction at that time, requires a stable team that knows they have an issue. With their eyes open to the issue, the team agrees that the team's goals are best served by not confronting the issue at this time. Rather than having the leader intervene (and choose the hammer size to be used), the team commits to addressing the issue during their normal flow of work. These team-led decisions can have less negative impacts overall and can be addressed successfully by a healthy team.

If the team is unsuccessful in dealing with the problem, the leader may address continuing issues using a smaller hammer approach. In order to maintain the positive momentum of the team, the leader can address 5% Dobermans in one-on-one or small group meetings. As with most one-on-one sledgehammer meetings, the leader is able to address the 5% Dobermans while avoiding the negative impacts a larger hammer approach has on the whole team.

Leadership Decisions

The remaining decisions regarding whether or not to intervene are judgement calls that test the leader's skills and relationship with their team. Part of this decision-making process involves the team itself. The quality of a team's internal relationships and the level of their ability to solve problems are key factors in deciding whether to intervene or let the team work through an issue. If a team member has previous unresolved behavior or commitment issues, the leader considers that fact in the decision. If prior issues reemerge, or team relationships suffer, it may be clear that an intervention by the leader will provide the best opportunity for a positive outcome. Whatever the factors, a decision must be made about whether or not to disturb the sleeping Doberman.

Facing issues directly. I choose to address every Doberman issue I believe has a chance to negatively impact my team presently or at any time in the future. Depending on the facts about the team and the Doberman situation, I make the decision about how to approach the problem. Whether it's me or a team that will be addressing the Doberman, careful planning and thorough, specific preparation is key for a successful meeting. Even experienced professionals use role playing to practice for a difficult conversation, and I often need to use several of *The Ten Tools* in order to resolve an issue.

One of the first steps I take when I decide to intervene is to consult with my mentors or supervisor (i.e. Marty, see Chapter 4). I listen to their advice and examples, and brainstorm possible strategies, reactions, and emotions that I should expect. Being aware of these Doberman-like behaviors helps me to effectively implement many of the strategies mentioned in *The Ten Tools*.

Let the team work it out. Some leaders take an enlightened and thoughtful approach to their leadership filter (see Chapter 3) when choosing to "wake the Doberman." For example, I know of leaders who have said, "I know [this situation] is here, but I don't think it will ever rise to the level of becoming a problem for our team." These leaders decide to not intervene, based on their instincts about the issues. If there are strong leaders within the team, or they have shown a clear commitment to the team's goals, the leader may give the team an opportunity to problem solve first before taking any action. At other times, the leader may be confident the issue will go away quickly without intervention or can be handled internally by the staff involved. Successfully working through issues can build trust within the team. Teams that become adept and comfortable with communication thrive on the synergy built by the trust and respect developed when they work through decisions together.

Though the leaders continue to monitor the issue in both of these situations, they don't engage with it. This application of the leadership filter allows these leaders to focus energy on other challenges. Again, as in the example above, if an individual or small group cannot solve their own problems after this approach, the leader can use 5% strategies to address their behavior immediately (see Chapter 4). However, teams that frequently rely on leader intervention in routine communication situations are often teams that have trust and confidence issues that may need to be addressed.

Ignore the problem. Ignoring a problem, or a pressing decision can also happen with a leader who is overwhelmed, stressed out, or mentally checked out. They may decide not to address a serious, sleeping Doberman issue because, "It's just not worth the hassle" or "[They] can't handle the stress right now." Ignoring serious issues is a problem, and teams can be negatively impacted by their leader's inability, or unwillingness, to act. This lack of action by the leader can have a negative impact on the leader and their team. What can be done to address the impacts on the team and/or the leader in such situations?

Changing my own behavior. Leaders might realize that they may ignore pressing issues because they are stressed out or not prepared. Even as an experienced leader, I need to monitor my own focus and energy levels when preparing to face Doberman situations. I need to guard against my own complacency. I can't take for granted that because I've had successful experiences with these situations in the past, I can now go into Doberman situations without careful preparation. I've made the mistake of not thoroughly preparing enough times to realize that I am more successful when my tools are sharp. The results are always better, and I've learned the time spent preparing saves time in the long run.

Some of the specific changes I've made to be better prepared for my Doberman conversations are shared in the following table (see Table 5.1).

Table 5.1
Preparing for Doberman Conversations

1. Make sure you have enough sleep

   ◊ I am a completely different person when I am rested, then when I'm fatigued.

1. Manage food and liquid intake

   ◊ Too much caffeine makes me jumpy and sometimes makes my chest tight.

      ■ I don't drink coffee before a presentation or a tough meeting.

   ◊ Don't overeat just prior to the conversation.

      ■ I plan to eat after the meeting.

      ■ Adrenaline and stress can upset your stomach.

1. Schedule the meeting

   ◊ I am sharpest and better rested in the mid-morning.

      ■ 10:00 AM is best for me because it allows me to take care of other morning issues so my brain is not multitasking during the meeting.

   ◊ If my conference is with educators, their teaching and coaching schedules will impact when the meeting will be.

      ■ If the meeting is with a group, if possible, I let them pick the time for the meeting - this prevents them from being upset with me before the meeting even starts.

      ■ Try not to schedule other stressful meetings immediately before or after your Doberman meeting.

      ■ Give your nervous system and adrenal gland a chance to settle back down.

1. Prepare to be successful

    ◊   Sharpen up your memory of the names of the people involved, even if they won't be at the meeting.

    ◊   Write down an agenda for how you want the meeting to proceed.

        ■   You won't share this agenda because you may change it several times during your meeting.

        ■   Use your agenda as a checklist so you can quickly refer to it during the meeting.

1. Prepare detailed speaking notes for every eventuality you can think of

    ◊   You can return to your notes when you get thrown off track.

    ◊   Highlight transition points.

    ◊   Write scripts for your major points of emphasis.

    ◊   Review your SIDWI skills from Chapter 1.

        ■   Plan ahead to listen, learn, transfer some power and solve the issue in the grey area.

        ■   Rattle the tablet.

    ◊   Review your hammer skills from Chapter 2- Sledge-hammer.

        ■   Plan to start with a medium sized hammer but be ready to increase hammer size if needed.

    ◊   Honor the 95% rule and include possible 5% meetings in your notes

1. Finish strong

    ◊   Don't lessen your impact with small talk at the end

Note: This table provides tips for facing Doberman conversations head-on. By following these tips, leaders can train themselves not to avoid these difficult confrontations that are a necessary part of leadership.

Staying sharp through mentoring. People who are in leadership roles some-times struggle with avoidance, as well. In this case, their supervisors might need to intervene. If the person who is not effectively handling parts of their job responsibilities is a school level principal or other administrative team leader, their supervisor needs to meet with them in private right away. Direct them to address the issues with their team immediately, while at the same time offering to help them prepare. Find out why this leader is not addressing these issues with the team. There are several common reasons I have observed, including; workload stress, lack of confidence, and lack of motivation.

If I thought the stress of their workload was preventing their success with their team, I may arrange to have some of their responsibilities taken off their plate temporarily. For example, I, or another district office administrator could complete observations and conferences with some of their staff. Another major stress reliever is to substitute at some evening events, especially at the high school level, since nighttime activities such as games, plays, concerts, and dances can take place up to six nights a week. Since other administrators might be attending many of these events anyway, they could easily help with student supervision.

I have also had team leaders who lacked confidence in their own abil-ity to handle tough meetings with their team. Encourage them to contact a mentor. If they don't have a mentor, I try to find a mentor for them that is a good fit, and if necessary, I mentor this leader myself. Mentoring sessions should focus on specific strategies to deal with the Doberman behaviors on their team. Share methods of preparing for Doberman conversations (listed in Table 5.1). As part of these specific skills, creating scripts to role play, such as those described in SIDWI and the 95% rule, could be helpful. Building tools to prepare for such meetings will improve their confidence and effec-tiveness. Make it clear to them that they have your support

Lack of motivation can also be a factor in a leader's willingness to address Doberman issues. Over my years as a leader in education, I was the direct super-visor for over 25 leaders who were in their last year before retirement. Most of these people were committed to finishing strong, but several, especially during the second half of the year, wanted to quit doing the difficult parts of their job. Because these were people I respected and had strong trust bridges with, addressing their behavior was something I never looked forward to. I met with each of them one-on-one and challenged them to go out strong. I was specific with what behavior I expected, and followed up with them regularly during the remainder of the year. All but one finished their year in an acceptable manner.

Four Categories of Dobermans

Dobermans come in all shapes and sizes. When a new leader enters a situation with an established team, they may face problems due to a lack of trust between the new leader and the team and reluctance of team members to change. The four types of Dobermans discussed in this section, the test driving Doberman, the chronically negative and/or sarcastic Doberman, the event-inspired Doberman, and the personal attack Doberman, push leaders to consider the various types of personalities and challenges that arise in team situations.

Many leaders are hired or promoted in order to initiate change in an organization. During the recruiting and hiring process, the needed changes are often laid bare to the team and the public. In many cases, this leader is hired to deal with some big Dobermans. In my experience as a new superintendent in three different districts, many teammates did not agree with the major changes sought by leadership, and I encountered test driving Dobermans, chronically negative and/or sarcastic Dobermans, event-inspired Dobermans, and personal attack Dobermans. While test driving Dobermans challenge a new leader, a chronically negative and/or sarcastic Doberman can cause strained relationships between the leader and staff members. When team members or a small group react to a decision, change, or reprimand, the event-inspired Doberman might result. Though these team members are usually supportive of the leader, a particular situation or event may cause Doberman-like reactions and emotions. Finally, the personal attack Doberman criticizes and attacks the leader without provocation. This Doberman dislikes the leader because of personal beliefs or issues, rather than actions the leader has taken. Each of the four Doberman reactions can produce differing responses. Table 5.2 breaks down each type by providing some common characteristics and responses.

Table 5.2
Specific Strategies for Four Types of Dobermans

1. The test driving Doberman
a. **Characteristics**
• common in new environments
• challenges your ability to do your new job
◊ probably tongue-in-cheek
◊ uses positive body language, humor
• wants to get acquainted with you
b. **Responses**
• expect that they'll greet you, so be prepared
• this is a bridge-building opportunity
• give them the benefit of the doubt
• use humor, small hammer approaches
• create positive, humble vibe, ask about their family
2. The chronically negative and/or sarcastic Doberman
a. **Characteristics**
• chronically negative, often has history
• long term negative impact on team
◊ team members have avoided or worked around them
◊ extra time and effort to complete projects
◊ loss of joy and spontaneity for the team
◊ may have had negative experiences with me or other bosses in the past

- may be impacted by negative life experiences off the job

b. Responses

- leader responds immediately at first manifestation of negative behavior

    ◊ first meeting is one-to-one, try to nip this in the bud

    ◊ start with medium sized hammer strategies

        - use direct, specific words and firm body language

        - clarity, "your behavior is unacceptable"

            o having a negative impact on the team's work environment

        - future occurrences will result in disciplinary action

        - provide written summary of the meeting with direct quotes

    ◊ keep your supervisor in the loop

    ◊ if negative behavior persists

        - move to heavier hammer strategies,

        - meet again immediately and provide written letter of reprimand, including future discipline options if the behavior continues

    ◊ if negative behavior lessens and/or if an effort is made to improve

        - meet to commend the efforts and results

        - move into small hammer strategies to discuss factors impacting the person

            o offer different types of support

            o employee assistance plan for counseling

            o teaming with a mentor

            o remind them they can meet with you at any time to support their efforts to improve

---

3. The event-inspired Doberman

---

a. **Characteristics**

- negative behavior often happens suddenly
- openly disagrees with a specific decision
    - ◊ may try to obtain support from colleagues
- may involve themself or be on behalf of a team member
- team may become divided into camps

b. **Responses**

- recognize emotions are high now, but they should subside with time
- meet with the lead Doberman first
    - ◊ start with small hammer strategies to gather information and keep your trust bridges intact.
    - ◊ be a listener, let them have their day in court
        - ■ make sure they realize you understand their position
        - ■ ask clarifying questions
        - ■ explain your rationale without violating confidentiality requirements
        - ■ create flow time opportunities
            - ○ "Let me have some time to think"
            - ○ "Can I get back to you next week?"
        - ■ be ready to firm up, if they don't decelerate
    - ◊ after providing flow time, provide a written summary, approved by your supervisor.
        - ■ Make sure the summary is "front page clean" which means the words selected are respectful to everyone and contain no exaggerations or stretches.

4. The personal attack Doberman

a. **Characteristics**

- can be mean spirited and sarcastic
- may bring up negative things from your past
- capable of spreading negative and untrue rumors
- may start unflattering nicknames
- spreads negative things to people who he knows may think it's funny

a. **Responses**

- focus on controlling your own emotions
    - ◊ use flow time to process your anger and frustration
- consult a trusted colleague or mentor
- use written notes when speaking
- use SIDWI skills - let them talk first, listen, learn, lead, patient, respectful
- stick to the facts
    - ◊ no wishful thinking or stretching the truth to make your point
- keep your conversation confidential
    - ◊ strong filter, don't spread unnecessary negatives
- check with your supervisor for input and to determine their support level of you on this issue

Note: This table summarizes characteristics and responses to four different types of Dobermans that are often encountered by leaders.

The Test Driving Dobermans

Test driving Dobermans are team members who challenge a new leader. In every leadership position, test driving Dobermans are vital to building the trust bridge with the new team. These Dobermans feel protective and territorial as they wait to learn about the new leader, much like a Doberman Pinscher who is on guard or has its hackles up. The test driving Doberman challenges the new leader's ability and effectiveness, usually through good natured barbs and humor that "test drive" the new boss's responses. At every opportunity, new leaders should trust the person or group's intentions are positive, and should try to turn these interactions into bridge-building opportunities. Test driving Dobermans can become friendly allies by following some simple strategies.

To give them the benefit of the doubt, assume they are kidding when they criticize your abilities, and assume they want to have a positive conversation and relationship with you. To accomplish this, use small hammer approaches, such as positive body language, including eye contact, smiling, gesturing, and leaning in to the conversation. Return their attempt at humor with humor of your own, including lots of laughter. I often said things like "Aw, come on. You have to at least give me a shot," or "Just because I'm not from [Montana, Idaho, or the middle school] doesn't mean I can't do a few things around here," or "You have such a great team here. Surely, you can carry me long enough for me to get a few clues." The goal is to create a vibe that is positive, humble, and somewhat self-deprecating. You want them to know you have a sense of humor, don't take yourself too seriously, and that you can take a punch.

Switch the focus of the conversation away from your abilities to building your personal relationship. Move into the grey area to begin some trust bridges. Ask about their families and what they like to do for fun. After every interaction, write down as many names, including family members, you can remember; I always carried paper and pen to catch the names while they were still fresh in my mind. By humanizing yourself to the team member, you can begin to build a relationship with them that allows them to see you as a person and not just the new leadership.

The Chronically Negative and/or Sarcastic Dobermans

The chronically negative and/or sarcastic team member can have a major harmful impact on the team in several important ways. When faced with these negative and sarcastic Dobermans, whether in a new setting or not, leaders must figure out how to change this person's behavior. There are often a few of these people within each team, which can cause the entire team to be less productive and less positive. Their negative behavior may be a result of a previous negative experience or disagreement with the current or past leader, supervisor, or teammate. It's also possible their negative approach is a result of other tough issues going on in their personal life that have no direct connection to the team. Though it may not be intentional, people who are enduring difficult life issues such as financial problems, illness, tragedy, or struggling personal relationships may take their pain and suffering to their job site.

Leaders coming into a new position may be faced with a general negativity that has been growing for years due to these different types of Dobermans. As teammates process their own negative emotions about job issues, they may talk with trusted colleagues and when those colleagues express support and empathy, the complainer (Doberman) can become emboldened. What started as a private conversation can spread until it becomes a serious problem for the leader and the team. Whether the chronically negative and/or sarcastic Doberman is a long-time faculty member on a team with a new leader, or a teammate the leader has known for years, use the one-on-one approach shared in the 5% section of the previous chapter. As a leader, your goal is to find the source of the negativity and address it as soon as possible. Use SIDWI strategies to create new trust bridges and move into the grey area to find solutions. You will learn again, that your insistence on dealing with tough, one-on-one conversations in a firm and decisive manner adds to your credibility as their new leader.

Negativity can inhibit the positive energy that drives strong teams. When one chronically negative and/or sarcastic Doberman is on the team, it can cause discomfort for the 95% of the team who is feeling positive. Those team members might avoid interacting with the negative people, which is an extra burden that can extend the time and effort needed for the team to reach its goals. The actions of such negative team members can create rifts on the team, resulting in weakened trust bridges.

The Event-Inspired Dobermans

Event-inspired Dobermans occur at times when a teammate or group disagrees with a certain decision or policy or when they feel like the leader is not listening to their opinion. The team member or small group might respond to a specific incident with negative emotions whereas this team member or group of people are positive the rest of the time.

Event-inspired Dobermans may appear when a decision impacts the team or when the team feels like their voice hasn't been heard. In the field of education, the time of year when I made decisions on teaching assignments, number of preparation periods, and room locations were the most emotion-packed times of the school year. It was during these weeks when event-inspired Dobermans often got their hackles up. Teaching a new grade level or adding new courses to prepare for meant added work for the teacher, so frustration and disappointment were both legitimate and understandable reactions. Even so, I needed to use small hammer strategies and one-on-one conversations with those impacted in order to rebuild a weakened trust bridge. Many times, teachers didn't feel like their preferences were being honored, but when I met with teachers individually, I was able to explain why a change was necessary. The conversation might not have always ended the way the teacher wanted, but by using SIDWI approaches, and strategies from Chapter 6, "You Can't Please Everyone, but You Can Treat Everyone Right", the teacher knew I had listened.

I also recall incidents when other teachers rallied around a colleague who had received a letter of reprimand or a disappointing evaluation. Though reprimands and evaluations were conducted with strict confidentiality, the impacted faculty often shared their emotional response with colleagues. As a result, the event-inspired Dobermans grew to a group of individuals rather than only one person. As the leader, I had to act quickly to reassure those who were upset and rebuild trust. Sometimes, this took time, but by being consistent with evaluations and policies, team members learned what they could count on with me and this created confidence in my decisions, albeit not always agreement.

The Personal Attack Doberman

As a leader, we sometimes face personal attacks from Dobermans, whose main goal is to cause pain to the leader as a result of an event or decision. These Dobermans are angrier and more aggressive than typical event-inspired Dobermans. These personal attacks are often not related to the leader's job performance or new rules. These attacks might result from a perceived slight to a person's belief system or personal hotspots (i.e. racism, sexism, and other issues of equity). The following example provides guidance for visualizing a personal attack Doberman scenario and strategies for tackling the issue.

Being chosen for the new position. Hiring decisions can be fertile sources for creating personal attack Doberman responses, and I experienced a Doberman attack when I was promoted for a position within the school district. My female co-worker resented that I was selected for a position that we had both applied for and publicly accused the school district of using sexism in their hiring practices, implying that I was chosen because I was a man—not because my qualifications were stronger. She considered appealing the decision, but decided to spread hateful rumors about me instead. These vicious rumors attacked my character and abilities. She started a rumor about my inability to accept umpire's calls when I was a coach. As the rumor spread, she wondered out loud what would happen if things didn't go my way as an administrator.

I felt personally attacked and emotional, close to losing my temper and confronting her. I briefly considered ways to get back at her in the same way she'd hurt me, but I knew that wasn't the right response. I knew I needed to take the higher road, and when I turned to two trusted colleagues, they convinced me to wait a couple days before deciding what to do. I remember one of them joking, "By the way, she is right about your temper with umpires, so I'd leave that one alone."

Their advice was perfect. As the weekend went by, I calmed down and realized the best approach was to not respond to her comments at all. I wrote some notes that helped me be prepared for any encounters with her rumors in the future. I also took my friend's advice and planned to respond to any umpire-related comments with humor, "I've learned a lot from those experiences." I prepared to use positive facial and body language, and speak in a calm, firm, and paced voice. I hadn't even started my new job yet, but this encounter provided a good lesson in dealing with personal attack Dobermans and learning to maintain my composure and emotions.

Table 5.3 describes strategies that can be used in personal attack situations. Remember, every challenging situation in your leadership position is an opportunity for growth. The more experience you get, your skills at conducting productive meetings and reacting to negative team members will become stronger.

Table 5.3
Tips for Dealing with Personal Attack Dobermans

1. Give yourself some flow time to calm down and get your thoughts together.

2. Show respect and remember your strong listening skills (SIDWI) and Ch. 6

   ◊ Be ready to exchange information and share power

   ◊ Don't make any commitments at a first meeting

      ▪ Develop your future comments or recommendations as you discover more information

      ▪ Don't be rushed into a spur of the moment response

3. Don't overreact by responding angrily, or making your own accusatory comments

4. Stay calm and patient, keeping both hands on the steering wheel is a sign of strength

5. Stick to the facts as you understand them. This is not a time for wishful thinking or stretching the truth to support your point of view.

6. Keep a tight Leadership Filter. Only share information with those who need it

7. Keep your supervisor in the loop and seek their input

   ◊ Find out what their support level is for your position

8. At future meetings, continue to stay calm and patient

   ◊ Don't overreact to comments about you, or your decisions

Note: Use the table above for strategies leaders can employ when dealing with personal attack Dobermans.

Using Doberman Strategies in Real Life

Being hired as a change agent can be a blessing and a curse, and I have personally learned and observed some important lessons on transition dynamics. The blessing of being promoted to a prestigious, new position where the top leaders provide latitude and authority, is that the new leader can implement new skills and strategies to accomplish the changes the top leadership prescribes. The curse is that these changes often need to be made quickly, during a one year "honeymoon period" and often include issues involving hiring, firing, and reassigning staff. Such emotional, public decisions often result in Doberman reactions from the individual and from sympathetic team members. The list of changes also routinely involves processes, protocols, and procedures that have become a way of life for team members. Many staff may resent the suggested changes and take them as an affront to their abilities and professionalism. Another challenge for new leaders is that despite changes that staff might feel angry and defensive about, the top leadership still expects an improvement to the overall culture of the workplace.

Whether a new leader comes into a new environment or is promoted from within, they must resist the temptation to act like they already know the answers about what is best for the team. The leader probably received information and heard opinions from the leadership team and other community members. What the leader needs to do now is to demonstrate commitment to understanding the team's point of view, including that of wounded team members. With transparency and consistency, the trust bridges necessary for change begin to form and strengthen. Consistent, positive body language and patient demeanor, understanding, and caring, thaw the battle lines, and the Dobermans begin to stop snarling. At every opportunity, I suggest using the human bridge-building skills described in the previous chapters.

Four Major Doberman Lessons From the Middle School

The following stories from my experience as a middle school principal share real life examples of dealing with multiple Dobermans at the same time. Though the Dobermans appeared in different forms and settings, the Doberman strategies in this chapter were effective in changing negative behaviors in each situation. Managing Dobermans by being willing to make high-stakes decisions achieved major cultural change.

I was caught by surprise the spring day when my superintendent informed me that I would be leaving my job as a high school counselor to become the principal at a grades 7-9 middle school in our district's lowest socioeconomic area. Over the years, I had heard legends about the Dobermans at my new school, but now it was time for me to learn about the legends for myself. My marching orders were clear— improve the school's culture, especially in the area of student discipline.

My new assistant principal was also a new administrator. Brooke was a highly talented and relational middle school teacher/coach and athletic director who had earned a reputation as an educator who really loved middle school kids. She taught me how you can have a heart of gold and a backbone of steel at the same time. She was a bridge-builder who could meet a kid right where they were, with exactly what they needed. Her loud laugh and sense of humor sent positive waves through the halls of our school every day of the week.

As we spent the summer meeting with staff, students, former students, and parents, we learned of four major challenge areas that needed to be addressed to change the culture in the school. Each challenge represented a Doberman described in this chapter. The first two Dobermans were the most challenging and were strongly connected. First, there was a decades old culture of physicality and intimidation. Fights were fierce and frequent, sometimes involving weapons. The second major Doberman was that the students were active in policing their own behavior at the school, using physical approaches to managing behavior that were not acceptable or effective. The two lesser Dobermans were reported as concerns by most every person interviewed over the summer. Because of constant issues with chewing gum being smashed on the floors, on the walls, and under the furniture, gum was forbidden within the school, and gum usage was a major factor in the school's discipline policy. The second lesser Doberman was the policy against wearing baseball hats in the school building.

Brooke and I knew trying to change any of these four Dobermans could result in an angry, defiant response from the students and the staff. We knew we needed to earn staff, parent, and student support to achieve a long lasting cultural change in the school, and we felt that minor tweaking of these four issues would not make the needed cultural change happen. Following is the account of how we attempted to address the four Dobermans standing in the way of accomplishing our marching orders for the coming school year.

We started with the two lesser Doberman issues (gum and hats) in order to begin building trust. Then, with the fragile trust bridges in place, we moved onto the more pressing issues of student discipline and self-policing.

SIDWI skills build trust bridges across age groups. As first time bosses of a team that was new to us, we held fast to our belief in the positive outcomes of SIDWI. Using SIDWI strategies to get some trust bridges started with the kids, Brooke and I proposed to change those two aforementioned school policies that had been major discipline issues at the school since the 1940's—no hats and no gum at school.

To address the antiquated rule that did not allow hats in the school or in the classrooms, we decided to completely flip the rule around. We stunned both the staff and student Dobermans in a positive way. The school colors were royal blue, white and red, and the school mascot was the Cubs so our school colors and mascot closely resembled those of the Chicago Cubs baseball team. With money donated by a booster and a huge discount from the owner of a local sporting goods store, we purchased 440 high quality, wool

Chicago Cubs baseball hats, one for each student and staff member at the school. The hats could be worn around school, and it was up to each teacher whether they could be worn in their classroom or not. If there were any problems with horseplay with the hats, the deal was off and the hats weren't allowed out of lockers during the school day for a week. Kids wrote their names in the bill of the hats with felt pens and took a lot of pride in their new hats. Many of the kids couldn't have afforded these nice hats, so they took special care of them, and we made a strong start toward building the trust bridges that gave us an actual chance to change the culture in their school.

The other policy we changed was allowing the kids to chew gum at school. In fact, we put gum in the school vending machines. The stipulation was that if there was any gum found stuck on the furniture or floor, the gum was off for a week. One of the 9th grade leaders suggested we also cut off the gum if any wrappers were found around the school, so we tacked that rule onto the policy, as well. Again, if teachers didn't want gum chewing in class, the kids just dropped the gum into the garbage can on their way into class. There was no longer a need to sneak the gum or hide it suddenly by sticking it on the floor or furniture.

We correctly predicted that these two rule changes were greeted with anger, resistance and disbelief by some staff and teachers on our team. Rather than giving in to adult outbursts, we decided to face their Doberman reactions with confidence that our decisions would benefit the entire school community. The staff and teacher Dobermans growled, "Harry, we know these kids," "You've gotta be nuts," and "All hell is going to break loose around here." Eventually, we won over the school staff and community and eliminated those two major discipline problems. Over a three year period, we needed to shut the gum off twice and never had to require hats in the lockers.

Quid pro quo and changing a discipline culture. Probably the only reason we didn't have a total staff rebellion over the rule changes that now allowed kids to wear hats and chew gum at school was the other side of the quid pro quo. Staff and student safety was challenge number one in our school. To answer that challenge, Brooke and I implemented a new set of discipline rules across the board, including much firmer, behavior expectations and consequences for the kids. Swearing in the halls or talking back to teachers resulted in in-school suspension (ISS) during lunch hour, with the number of days based on the specific behavior. Having ISS during lunch was especially effective because students loved their chance to hang with their friends during lunch. Verbal threats or verbal bullying resulted in after-school study suspension which meant the kids missed their after school activities during their suspensions.

The most impactful discipline change quickly put a damper on the number of fights. The new fighting rule was very straightforward. If you closed your fist and struck another student, you were suspended out of school (OSS) for at least three days and could not be on school grounds during the suspension. Days could be added depending on the intensity of the fight. One aspect that increased the impact of OSS was that parents became more intimately involved in changing their student's behavior. The family impact of arranging supervision for their child during the OSS was a strong motivator to change a child's behavior. News of a student's OSS spread pretty quickly around the community, and most families were embarrassed to have their son or daughter out of school.

The quid pro quo was clearly understood by the students. The students talked about how the new hat and gum policies made them feel trusted and respected by the adults in the school. Among the students, there was a strong feeling of "we don't want to lose these new freedoms," and the staff reported a clear improvement in student attention and behavior in their classrooms. Many parents called or stopped by to tell us how their child's whole attitude had changed toward school and how they were now actually doing their homework.

There's a fight down in the wing. Brooke and I had decided to wait about a month to let the kids have their first afternoon school dance. We needed that time to get our own feet on the ground with the kids and the staff. The kids had been awesome for that first month, and they were totally excited about the dance. The dance had gone off without a hitch until about 15 minutes before the bell that ended the school day. With the music blaring, one of my teachers ran up and shouted in my ear, "There's a fight down in the wing." My heart pounded as I ran with Brooke and a couple of teachers to the wing. There was a girl knocked out, lying on her back on the floor, with another girl cradling her head. Eight kids were standing in a circle around her, and none of them appeared to be upset.

I looked around the circle and demanded, "Who did this?" At that moment, a ninth grade boy, who I already knew the staff thought of as a leader in the school, looked at me and respectfully said, "Mr. Amend, we take care of these things around here." I knew that changing this self-policing tradition was sure to be one big, angry Doberman. None of the kids in the circle admitted who the assailant was. The girl had regained consciousness and was now standing on her feet. The bell ending the dance and the school week rang, and the students headed for their lockers and the buses. Brooke calmly said, "I'll find out who did this," and walked up the hall. By the time our girl's counselor and I had walked the girl to the office, Brooke was waiting with the name of the assailant. A group of students who trusted her, who appreciated their safer school, and who wanted to do the right thing had told her about the fight and all the details leading up to it. Over the next few months of tighter enforcement of discipline rules, most of the students were glad to relinquish their self-policing roles. We still had to keep a close eye on a few 9th graders, but by the time we started school the following fall, the discipline baton had been passed from the students back to the adults.

Over my three years at the middle school, the students showed me what it meant for adults and students to build strong trust bridges with each other. I met some scary Dobermans and learned many important lessons about different types of power from both my staff and our students. I often learned it was easier to build trust bridges with a middle school student than with a staff or community member. Those three years at the middle school served as a further reinforcement of my belief in SIDWI.

Conclusion

This chapter provided examples and suggestions for dealing with people's emotional reactions to decisions or policy changes in the workplace. By identifying the reason behind the reaction, leaders can move toward solving the problems and soothing the Dobermans that arise. As a reminder, Doberman Pinchers are loyal, loving dogs, but when they are startled or provoked that loyalty can often result in protectiveness, fearfulness, and aggression. When facing Doberman reactions in the workplace, I hope the Doberman analogy will grow to be a useful way of recalling the skills and information addressed in this chapter.

Please use Table 5.3 to brainstorm major concepts from the chapter. Identify two strategies you can use to deal with Dobermans on your teams. These strategies could be specific for certain types of Dobermans identified in the chapter, such as event-inspired Dobermans, chronically negative Dobermans, test driving Dobermans, or personal attack Dobermans. As you consider strategies presented, you may also connect these strategies to ideas presented in earlier chapters in the book.

Table 5.3
Action Plan: Don't Kick a Sleeping Doberman

What are two takeaways from this section? 1. 2.
What two strategies will you use to practice dealing with negative reactions on your team? 1. 2.
What steps will you take now? (Action Step for Don't Kick a Sleeping Doberman)

Note: This table provides readers with an opportunity to apply lessons learned about knowing how and when to deal with potentially difficult, emotional reactions on a team

CHAPTER 6

TOOL #6: YOU CAN'T PLEASE EVERYONE, BUT YOU CAN TREAT EVERYONE RIGHT

"You Can't Please Everyone But You Can Treat Everyone Right" expands on some of the key conversation skills (listening, learning, and leading) explored in the first five chapters. While many of the strategies and stories in previous chapters dealt with addressing problem employees or discipline situations, Chapter 6 adopts a focus on counseling concepts, the power of listening, and strategies for partnerships between the leader and team members. Leadership actions and words that support growth are almost all small hammer strategies (see Chapter 2), and belief, patience, and persistence create opportunities for growth in one-on-one, small group, and larger team settings. In this chapter, I share key counseling concepts, such as having high expectations, listening carefully, providing flow time, and cultivating positive relationships with the public—concepts I learned while in my role as a school administrator, counselor, teacher, and coach. Personal examples shared in this chapter help to illustrate how adopting a growth mindset helps to build the team and its trust bridges.

The Power of High Expectations

Success is a mindset, and the parable of "Jane's Fourth Grade Miracle" provides an example of the leader's power to help their team to exceed expectations (see Figure 6.1).

Figure 6.1
Jane's Fourth Grade Miracle

On Friday evening, Jane got a call from her local school district congratulating her, and informing her that she had just been selected for the new fourth grade teaching opening. The first day of class was Monday and Jane could come to the school over the weekend to pick up her class list and decorate her classroom if she wished. There were twenty four students in her ethnically diverse class. As Jane looked over her class roster, she noticed that all of her students had an IQ between 130 and 155. Jane felt flattered that as a first year teacher, she had been selected to teach such an advanced class.

Jane immediately got online and started purchasing and developing enrichment activities to supplement the district's fourth grade curriculum. As her first year flew by, Jane's students accepted every challenge and thrived. At her year-end evaluation conference, Jane was surprised when she walked into the principal's office, and the district superintendent was also seated at the office table. The superintendent spoke first. "Jane, I asked to attend your conference because I wanted to meet you personally. I know you are a first year teacher, and I wanted to hear directly from you, what you had done this year, to bring about this extraordinary achievement by all twenty four students in your class. Your class has some of the highest Fourth Grade Test scores in the state."

Jane replied, "When I looked at my class roster and realized that every one of my students was gifted, I knew I had to work extra hard and provide enrichment materials to stretch them and motivate them. Every day I reminded them that I knew how smart they were and that I expected them to do their very best." With a puzzled look on her face, the superintendent gazed over at the principal, who returned her gaze, with a look of wonder of his own. After a long and awkward pause the principal asked Jane, "What made you think that these kids were gifted?" Jane pulled the class gradebook out, and opened it on the table in front of the two administrators. With her finger, she ran down the list of the student IQ's next to each student's name. The IQ's were all between 130 and 155, the genius level, for every student in the class.

With tears welling up in his eyes, the principal began to weep softly. He knew full well that many of these students were from poor or dysfunctional families. He also knew some of these students had struggled mightily and had little or no success in school until this 4th grade year. The principal also knew eleven of these students had been "frequent flyers" in the school discipline system. He had checked and confirmed, and not one of these students had a discipline referral this year, even from their PE class. In a halting voice, the principal said, "Jane, those numbers next to the student's names are their locker numbers," at which time the superintendent began to weep openly.

Note: I have heard this parable, but haven't seen it published. The story as written above is from my memory.

The two experienced administrators in the story could have been weeping for a number of reasons. Experienced teachers and administrators often observe students who suffer from malnutrition, lack of sleep, and frayed relationships in the family. To see a group of at-risk students respond so well because their teacher had a stubborn belief they could succeed was an exciting moment in the career of any veteran educator. The principal and superintendent could have been touched by the sincerity and innocence of a young teacher who was committed enough to challenge her students to excel. It's also possible the administrators were crying because this rookie teacher brought nothing but the best to her students for 180 days and it impacted their performance in a magnificent way.

Jane's grit, determination, and attention to detail helped her fourth graders become top performers. Her story shows the power a leader's careful observation and individualized treatment can have. Her daily care and nurturing of every child in her class stayed steadfast, especially early in the year when trust bridges were just beginning. As mutual trust grew, the students adjusted to their teacher's high expectations. Jane was in it for the long haul, and as trust bridges with each student strengthened, the students became empowered. Jane's strong and steady belief became the fuel that powered her students' success. Believing she had been given a class of gifted students, Jane was not aware of her students' past negative school experiences or their homelife traumas. The fact that these students had struggled mightily during their first four years of school made the prognosis for success in their fourth grade year in Jane's class even more bleak, yet they succeeded and exceeded expectations—scoring among the highest fourth graders in the state. Jane's high expectations made all the difference.

The Power of Listening

"I don't know if they agreed with me,
but at least they heard me out.
I was respected, and I was treated right."

Whether with a family member, a teammate, or any other person, the above quote should be a goal for every conversation. Leaders must be committed to investing time listening and building strong trust bridges from the very beginning of relationships and continuing to strengthen those bridges over time. Time spent building and maintaining early trust bridges will make up for the time and hardship of trying to fix problems caused by the lack of trust bridges later.

One of the best ways to build credibility as a leader is to take the time to be a careful listener. Always remember that two very important outcomes are guaranteed every time you listen to another person. (1) Before even opening your mouth, the other person is validated and empowered. The act of taking time (being patient) and using key listening skills to hear the person out (e.g. not interrupting) affirms them and builds their trust. (2) As you focus, take notes, and ask probing questions, you also learn more about the person, and information that can improve trust bridges.

Over the course of my career, I realized an important fact— in many cases, the person speaking to me wasn't even seeking a specific outcome, they just wanted to be respected and heard. During my formative years as a leader, I also learned that key listening skills and hammer selection skills were just as important in my everyday leadership role, as they were during times of crisis.

Chapter 1 (SIDWI) includes detailed tips to promote excellent listening. Though SIDWI strategies were provided in the context of difficult conversations, team leaders can build trust in all situations with team members simply by listening carefully. Behaviors such as focused eye contact, forward leaning, and positive affirmation are keys to earning trust. Trust bridges can be built during both tough and easy times. Your attitude of patience and interest, including asking probing questions and taking notes, also increases the comfort level and confidence of the person you are speaking with.

When a leader takes the time to listen to others, the benefits outweigh the time spent from the daily hourglass. Keeping the hourglass in mind, leaders who take the extra time and effort to be great listeners may need to prioritize other tasks or decide to work late, through lunch, or on the weekends to make up the time spent listening. But the time spent listening is time spent gluing popsicle sticks on trust bridges. The added insight gained by listening to a teammate and getting to know their passions, values, and priorities enriches the leader as much as it empowers the teammate. As the leader's reputation for being a careful and caring listener spreads to the team, students, and community members, the communication lines stay open, and the trust bridges stay strong.

The Power of Flow Time

As mentioned earlier (see Chapter 1 and Chapter 5), the proper use of flow time can be a key ingredient in successfully handling tough emotional situations— but what exactly is flow time? Flow time means allowing an individual or group of people time to process a difficult situation in their own way and on their own timeline.

From the beginning, this book has focused on the importance of managing time when building trust bridges. Listening skills and patience are small hammer, bridge building strategies. There have been times during my career when people have been angry with me. They promised to "come down to my office and give me a piece of their mind"— but, what started as rage on Monday, was more manageable on Tuesday, and often became a source of laughter by Friday. Flow time allowed them to evaluate the outcome of their actions, giving them a chance to calm down, to think, and to talk to people they trust. In these cases, time itself became the intervention, and the situation resolved itself.

One question that new leaders often ask is— "when do I need to provide flow time?" The most common reason for trying to create flow time is when emotions seem too high and they realize that the best chance at reaching a strong solution is allowing those high emotions to calm down. In flow time situations, leaders avoid intervening unless it becomes necessary. If the leader feels the other party needs some flow time to stop and think, the leader should have that person schedule the next meeting at a time they feel it is necessary. This allows that person as much time as they need to think about and control their feelings. However, if the leader is the one needing the flow time to think and plan, then the leader can set up the follow-up meeting. In prolonged situations, leaders may combine the strategies of using flow time, while touching base with the person (or group) periodically during the process. Such situations could include grieving after a tragedy, or needing some more planning time or committee work when considering a major change. The need for this combined approach could be suggested by either or both sides and may also be planned in advance of starting the meeting process.

Once a leader knows that flow time is necessary, there are a few ways to create that time. As mentioned in Chapter 1, purposely taking a break in the middle of a difficult meeting can create flow time for participants to process their feelings and thoughts. When necessary, create flow time by saying such things as, "There's a lot to chew on here. Can you check back with me tomorrow (or next week)?" or "There are a lot of pieces to this puzzle. Can you call me next week if you want to take a further look at it?" These statements tell the person that their concern is a big deal to you and you need more time to think about it. If the irate person is on the phone, say, "I'm busy right now. Let's set up a time to talk tomorrow (preferably in person)." This might frustrate the person at the time, but it forces them into flow time and creates a better opportunity for the leader to plan for effective strategies to deal with the situation. To begin using this strategy, new leaders need to plan for breaks to increase the possibility of situations (and time) flowing more naturally and calming down without intervention. Taking some time to think about the issue can lessen emotions surrounding the situation. Don't plan to make any commitments, statements, conclusions, or resolutions until after the flow time period.

It is often true that people who are emotionally charged, don't want any flow time. When people won't calm down, the leader may need to use a large hammer approach, by insisting on a break. Such words as, "I think we need to take a break right now and set up a time to continue our conversation tomorrow." or "I have another commitment, and I'm already running late, so let's set up a time to meet tomorrow to continue our conversation." These statements need to be accompanied by insistent body language such as a firm voice, eye contact, and a stern facial countenance. By suggesting the meeting later, the leader sends a strong message that the issue is important and they aren't just trying to avoid working toward a solution. The overnight delay allows time for the participants to consult other people and, hopefully, get a chance to calm down. If the person can't meet the next day, schedule the next meeting as soon as both calendars allow— additional days for flow time could actually benefit the outcome of the conflict.

The Power of Public Relations

For the purpose of this section, "public" is defined as any person or group of people that is outside of the immediate team. For a large company, it could mean other departments, branches, or the company's administrative hierarchy. For any school, it could be staff, family members, individuals from the community, or a main street business. In a larger school district, public could mean other schools or departments within the district. Earning trust with any of these public entities requires the same building blocks discussed in the first five chapters of this book. Building and maintaining trust bridges with different public groups is vital to success as a business, school, and family leader.

Staff, students, customers, and voters will often want to know their leader's opinions on issues that are important to them. In the education environment, areas that draw special interest from the public may be student and staff supervision or the leader's level of focus and support for specific curriculum offerings and co-curricular activities such as music, drama, clubs, and sports. Because a leader plays a major role in creating, delivering and implementing the team's public messaging, while considering the message being sent to the public, leaders should ask themselves:

- Am I willing to embrace and support those public values?

- Do I clearly communicate with the public(s)?

- Do I hold open houses, forums and/or events that invite people to become more familiar with my team's mission, goals and needs?

- Do I make it a priority to be visible and get personally involved in important community events or efforts?

- Have I taken the time to learn about the public's history and value systems?

- How can I create shared goals between the public(s) and my team?

- How do I create strong trust bridges between the public(s) and my team?

- How do I make commitments that are realistic and fulfill those promises in a reasonable timeline?

The above questions are not listed in chronological order or in order of importance, but each of these questions pushes the leader to consider how actions and communication impacts the public's perception of the leader and the organization. Some of these questions ask the leader to take steps toward getting involved with the public(s) by going above and beyond; others simply remind the leader of areas to think about regarding responsibilities toward the public(s). Whether speaking with someone personally, through a video, or being observed at an event, remember that your facial and body language will always be a large part of what is remembered.

Strong public relations are a key to building trust in any school district, business enterprise, or even family situations. The power of public relations lies with a consistent and persistent, accurate message delivered and acted upon. Written messages create a reliable, common voice and provide clarity. A well-worded and accurate written message can be a strong bridge-builder for your team and for your public(s). An important role of a leader is to make sure the team has received, and always understands, what the team message is, and what the message is not. The clarity of the message is especially important when changes are being made. Clear written communication can prevent an overzealous team member from unwittingly damaging the credibility of the whole team with inaccurate information.

Using the "Powers" with Diverse Teams

The two stories that follow illustrate the bridge building challenges and strategies explored in this chapter, including high expectations, listening, flow time, and public relations. Reflecting back on these experiences, I was able to make strong connections to the Chapter 6 tool, "You Can't Please Everyone but You Can Treat Everyone Right." These experiences solidified the importance of this concept to creating a strong team.

It Takes Time to Build a Trust Bridge with a Roughneck

"It Takes Time to Build a Trust Bridge with a Roughneck" focuses on how a team of former education leaders (i.e. retired principals and superintendents) used the power of flow time and listening skills to train a team of leaders in the energy field (i.e. supervisors, managers, and leaders of an oil company).

My education team had been hired to train the energy team in leadership skills before they headed for the isolated oil fields in Northern Alberta. Ironically, this three-year experience not only taught the energy leaders new leadership skills, the education team also polished up leadership skills during the experience. The energy team's diversity (i.e. ethnicity, spoken languages, education levels, communication styles, and social mores) presented multiple challenges for both teams. Creating, monitoring, and adjusting flow time became a constant challenge, and from start to finish, every listening skill explored in this book was used, and improved on. The energy team's ability to learn leadership skills, including flow time and listening skills, turned out to be key factors in their success in their rugged new environment.

Though the four of us on the education team had different styles, our combined 130+ years as educators had prepared us for this new bridge-building challenge. The original plan was to train the 70 members of the management team, but we ended up training all 200 team members. We first embedded with the team in Calgary for six months, getting to know the team and writing/compiling the training materials. During those months, we worked one-on-one and in small groups with our energy partners, and we began building trust bridges using many of the listening skills explored in *The Ten Tools*. Flow time and patience became constants during these early conversations as we listened and took notes, learned more about energy culture, and built relationships. We learned their acronyms and language patterns, and they learned ours.

When it was time for the training to start, the 223-page, 3-day training binder was well-received, but we soon learned that creating the binder was the easy part. The training classes ranged in size from 8-30 participants which were small enough groups to use *the ten tools* in conversations, but large enough to also require tools to manage group dynamics. As each of our team began teaching the lesson we'd prepared, it became clear that our energy partners had not gone into this field to spend time in a classroom. It was during the first classes that our training team honed its listening skills and flow time strategies. We became notetakers as they responded to our probing questions. We also used patient, positive, and inviting body language such as eye contact, hand gestures, and nodding to encourage our energy partners to continue sharing. We became proficient at using group flow time when it became clear they needed a break, even if it was unscheduled. Because 30% of the team spoke English as a second language and their ability to communicate varied widely, we used plenty of communication strategies (i.e. extra flow time, eye contact, listening) to support their learning.

Our team continued to learn cultural realities as the training progressed. The energy partners' sense of humor was often rough and tumble, no holds barred, and no one was excluded, especially us. For example, we provided breakfast and lunch each day, and though we were not responsible for the menu, we received quick and harsh feedback the first time a meal showed up without meat. The first time we tried to delay a smoke break, they just laughed, got out of their chairs, and left the room.

We learned that most of these leaders would rather spend 60 hours on a wellhead in frigid conditions than spend 30 minutes conducting an annual evaluation conference with one of their direct reports. It was our job to teach them the listening skills, the SIDWI techniques, and especially the hammer strategies for having these difficult conversations. Role playing these new skills was a necessary part of the training, and though their non-verbal and verbal feedback made it clear they didn't like it, they worked hard and got a lot out of role playing. Many guys referred to actually practicing these techniques, as the most important part of the training for them.

Patience was at a premium as we witnessed the heart and passion of these tough guys every day. Taking time to learn their culture, vocabulary, and acronyms showed them we cared. All of these factors served as the Elmer's glue in building trust bridges capable of creating new relationships and new learning. As the energy team learned to lead through our training and modeling, we marveled at the power of *The Ten Tools* in growing their skills and confidence level in their new leadership responsibilities.

Would You Like that Happy Meal Supersized, Sir?

"Would You Like that Happy Meal Supersized, Sir?" is the story of a young lady who used high expectations, listening skills, and strong public relations strategies to build successful teams in two very different job settings. In the story below, readers learn how Sherry applied skills she developed while managing a successful McDonald's restaurant to the field of education, becoming one of the top high school principals in the United States. One of the key lessons from Sherry's story is that a set of high quality leadership tools is transferable, which is an important consideration for any aspiring leader.

After teaching a year of secondary school math and coaching basketball, Sherry traveled for five years while her husband Josh pursued a career as a military officer. Sherry worked in the McDonald's restaurant system during their travels, and then in 1981, Josh and Sherry took out a loan, bought a lot, and built a McDonald's on the Montana Hi-Line. As Josh continued to travel and finish up his career, Sherry stayed in Montana, opened the new restaurant, and finished her Masters degree in guidance and counseling. After supervising the construction, Sherry recruited, hired, and trained all of her employees from the local talent pool. She spent the next 12 years leading a team that was regularly recognized by the McDonald's Corporation for its excellence.

From the day of her very first employee training, Sherry clearly communicated high expectations to every member of her team. Though her team included employees of all ages and genders, her high expectations applied to every employee. Whether the teammate was a high school dropout, a retired professional, a single parent, or a teenager working after school, Sherry believed in them and in their ability to do their job and be an excellent teammate, and she stayed consistent with her belief in them, even during the tough times.

A core value of the McDonald's corporation is their strong public relations focus. Sherry built and nurtured her team in every aspect of public relations. Staff training along with consistent, swift follow-up to correct or congratulate team members was a hallmark of Sherry's McDonald's management. Knowing your audience and providing what they wanted in a quick, accurate, and positive way was a habit and behavior pattern that every team member could achieve.

Over the years, Sherry hired many team members. Some were painfully shy, some were in their first job, and some had disabilities. Because of Sherry's supportive culture, driven by consistent daily affirmations, one-on-one coaching, and consistent positive reinforcement, new teammates settled in, gained confidence, and developed positive habits and skills that lasted a lifetime. When personal challenges occurred, such as pregnancies, health problems, or family issues, Sherry stood by her employees and helped them through those tough times.

In 1993, Sherry and her husband sold the restaurant and returned to Northwest Montana. Sherry got a job working as a high school guidance counselor and teacher. When I arrived as the new superintendent of the school district, Sherry was finishing her first year as an assistant principal at the high school.

My first order of business in my superintendent role was to hire the replacement for the recently vacated high school principal position. In order to provide a broad range of staff and community input, I selected a hiring committee of 17 people. The committee brainstormed a list of characteristics to use during the screening process: honest, caring, patient, organized, clear, candid, predictable, attentive, prepared, and thoughtful. There were over 20 applicants for the position, including well regarded, experienced candidates from within the district and around the country. Sherry made the list of five interview candidates.

I didn't know Sherry at that point, but as she began to speak, she had a slight smile and spoke with a strong voice. She had a dry sense of humor, and several times as she answered questions, she told funny stories about McDonald's, herself, and her physical size. Considering Sherry was so small in physical stature (only 5'1"), I smiled to myself as I imagined her walking around the high school with the three large men who would be working as assistant principals. I can still recall members of the committee laughing so hard we had to wait to ask the next question.

With every question, she stepped slightly toward the person asking the question, looked them directly in the eye, and told a story that answered the question. Every answer worked its way back around to high expectations and taking care of people. She had spent 12 years caring for, molding, and growing at-risk team members of every age into successful, happy people. She had a strong flavor of holding people accountable while causing them to grow. At McDonald's, Sherry handled every personnel and public relations problem herself. It was one of those interviews where she didn't once have to say what she would do—she could always say what she had done.

After Sherry's interview several committee members joked that a 12-year career running a McDonald's might be a great way to prepare for the principal's job at a large high school, and Sherry was selected for the job. During her six years as principal at the high school, she performed strongly in each of the character traits the hiring committee had been looking for. High expectations became a constant for every staff member and student. Her public relations skills quickly became legendary with the students, staff, and the community. Her insistence on careful planning and accurate, timely follow through were appreciated and respected. Her predictability and consistency in student and staff management issues quickly added to her credibility as staff, students, and parents learned how she responded to a given issue. As she earned the reputation for being a patient, careful listener, Sherry built trust bridges, and her trust empowered administrators and staff on her team to do their jobs and to develop their own leadership skills. With a culture based on high expectations for every teammate and student, a feeling of empowerment and inspiration, and strong public relations, the staff and students at Sherry's school experienced great success.

Eventually, Sherry was asked to be the planning principal for a new high school in the district, and after eleven award winning years as the principal there, Sherry was again promoted, this time to the position of assistant superintendent for the entire district. In this position, the district and community continue to benefit from her high expectations and public relations skills, as she currently serves in this position at the time of this book's publication. Her impact as a leader who excels in high expectations, listening skills, and public relations resulted in success for many of the leaders she nurtured. In fact, five of her assistant principals became principals, and two of her protégés became superintendents.

Conclusion

The commitment of the leader to maintain high expectations, develop strong listening skills, use flow time effectively, and grow strong public relationships is a starting point for building trust bridges. Treating people right creates confidence and self-esteem in a team. When the boss believes in their team's ability and takes the time to care and listen, the team stays focused on their goals. The boss's use of high expectations, careful listening, flow time, and strong public presence sends the message that they care and respect their team, which motivates a team to higher performance levels in both classroom and business settings. Over time, by practicing the "powers" discussed in this chapter, the leader will create and sustain the stable, predictable, and safe work environment that teammates covet.

In Table 6.1, leaders are tasked with considering ways to treat their teams right and build strong trust. Using strategies to create high expectations, strong listening skills, and flow time can create stronger relationships with the team and the public. By considering the strategies in this chapter, leaders can create stronger relationships with their teams and stakeholders.

Table 6.1
Action Plan: You Can't Please Everyone But You Can Treat Everyone Right

What are two takeaways from this section?   1.   2.
What two strategies will you use to practice the powers of high expectations, listening, flow time, or public relations?   1.   2.
What steps will you take now? (Action Step for You Can't Please Everyone...)

Note: This table guides the reader to further explore ways to value and respect people even if you don't agree with them. As with SIDWI, treating people with respect builds trust bridges and stronger relationships with the team.

CHAPTER 7
TOOL #7: DON'T SAY "UTILIZE"

"Don't Say 'Utilize'" focuses on the importance of careful preparation and choosing the right vocabulary and delivery style for your audience. Whereas the first several chapters of this text spelled out different vocabulary and non-verbal methods for succeeding in one-on-one and small group, bridge-building conversations, Chapter 7 focuses on public speaking. Coming from a teaching and coaching background, I'd become comfortable in front of smaller groups, but as I began climbing the leadership ladder, I found I was often expected to speak to larger audiences, including the public at-large. As was true when I switched vocabulary and presentation approaches between teaching senior boys English, coaching a baseball team, working with rough-necks in Canada, or teaching a graduate university class, I discovered the need to tailor my preparation, vocabulary, and delivery style to the purpose and the audience in these larger group opportunities.

This chapter begins by exploring the importance of being prepared for your speech. The following section explores strategies on how to tailor vocabulary to your audience, including when to use two-bit or two-buck words and the impact these types of words can have on different audiences. Gaining the skills to be nimble and versatile when changing audiences or topics will also be covered in these strategies. Regardless of the audience, your body language and physical cues can have a major impact on the message you seek to deliver. The final instructional section of the chapter focuses on how using lingo, initials, and acronyms can be conversation and comprehension stoppers.

Careful Preparation and Practice

Public speaking is often referred to as people's number one fear— and for good reason. Over the years, I have heard some great speeches and some not so great. I've learned from famous athletes, entertainers, politicians, and experts who were paid $100,000 for a 30 minute speech. I've listened to keynote speakers who were experienced and engaging— I have also experienced speeches from those who were senile or drunk. I've lost count of the times when a speaker read from notes in a monotone voice. I've heard profane language at a church conference and inappropriate jokes and humor at virtually every type of conference. I was even in the audience when a speaker gave the wrong speech because his assistant put the wrong notes in his briefcase.

Over the years, I've attended, been a speaker at, or presided over conferences, classes, and events of many kinds. I learned that careful preparation and practice are as important with larger group presentations as they are with tough one-on-one conversations. Public speakers appear calm and confident in front of a large group after putting in the hours of necessary preparation and practice. National conferences such as the American Association of School Administrators (AASA), the National School Boards Association (NSBA), and the National Association of School Principals Conference (NASSP) often draw over 10,000 attendees. The number of people in a large audience can be intimidating for an unseasoned speaker, but even the most dynamic speakers usually have notes they can refer to at any time during their speech. Many speeches in front of large groups are recorded for a video record, which might add to the stress for any speaker.

In Table 7.1, I share some of the ways I prepare for a major speech, including steps that will take you from a blank page to the day of your presentation.

Table 7.1
Tips for Preparing a Presentation

Prior to writing your speech:

• Confirm the exact subject area of your speech and how your presentation will fit in with other items (i.e. speeches, classes, breakout sessions) on the conference agenda
 	
    ◊   This step will avoid repetition between other presentations
 	
• Check how much time you have to give your speech
 	
• Check the availability of audio-visual equipment and support personnel
 	
    ◊   Prepare your speech to match your time slot
 	
    ◊   Don't exceed your time allocation
 	
• Confirm the details about printing and copying any handouts, binders, or other materials
 	
    ◊   Who will be paying for materials?
 	
    ◊   Who is responsible for organizing the materials?
 	
    ◊   How will materials be distributed (i.e. handed out, on the tables or seats)?
 	
• Allow enough time to thoroughly research your topic
 	
• Remember the PURPOSE of your speech

Writing your first draft:

• Start your first draft as early as possible in order to give yourself time to set it aside and even "sleep on it" during your preparation
 	
• List the tentative title and key topic areas of your speech
 	
    ◊   Type a double-spaced narrative of what you want to say for each of the key topic areas
 	
    ◊   Double spacing leaves room for you to write between the lines of your draft as you edit

- Decide how to "open" the speech

    ◊ From your entire draft, select an introductory paragraph that you think will hook your audience's interest

    ◊ Starting a major speech with a joke or funny (you hope) story is risky and I don't recommend it.

- Write a conclusion that will grip your audience and cause them to remember your speech.

- Create smooth transitions between the main ideas

Revising your draft:

- Some speakers like to rehearse their speech in front of someone they trust during the early stages to get input on the content.

    ◊ You can ask that person which parts of your speech seemed most relevant and memorable.

    ◊ Read your entire speech, with pauses, and time it. Is the speech too long or too short for the time slot?

    ◊ You will need to add or remove details and/or stories if necessary to adjust the time frame.

- Write keywords in the margins of the draft to identify the main ideas and key points.

    ◊ This technique can be useful when you need to shorten your speech and sticking to the key idea will allow you to delete some less important words

- This writing key words in the margin technique also adds to your organization.

    ◊ A delivery that is too loosely organized, can lead to rambling

    ◊ Poorly organized speeches require the audience to try to organize the main ideas, which impacts their comprehension of the message.

Practicing your speech:

• Start timing your rough draft with a stopwatch so you can stop and regroup during your early practicing
 	
• If your speech is longer than 10 minutes, don't try to memorize it word for word.
 	
• Memorize your transitions and other key focus points so you can step away from your notes (wander) during those times to connect in a tighter way with your audience
 	
    ◊ Practice any words, tone, or body language you will use to create the connection between the ideas
 	
• Each section of your speech will be its own story, practice telling these stories, not word for word
 	
• From the beginning of your preparation, mark your script with spots where you will use physical cues and/or enhanced body language to get your message across.
 	
    ◊ As with one-on-one or small groups, direct eye contact, facial expressions and head movement can add to the impact of your words
 	
        ■ Following a particularly powerful speech, I have heard members of large audiences say they felt the speaker was talking directly to them because of their strong eye contact.
 	
    ◊ Hand gestures such as palms up and motioning with, and pointing your finger can express excitement or wonder
 	
    ◊ Moving around the stage or room can increase energy, and closer proximity to the audience can bring a stronger focus.
 	
• After you have read your draft several times, continue practicing telling your stories without your notes.
 	
• Highlight on your draft, areas that you want to emphasize in each story. Every time you reread and retell your story, you will remember more details
 	
• Practice your speech in front of a mirror and focus on your facial body language and physical cues mentioned above in this table.

◊ Plan to speak with a relaxed positive facial expression unless you intentionally want to change your facial expression for impact

- Time your speech exactly, both reading it and rambling a bit through it

◊ Find your happy medium

Five minutes before your speech:

- Visit a restroom well before you go to the microphone.

- Check your teeth and face.

- If you're wearing slacks, remove the contents of your pockets.

- Make sure your shirt/blouse is tucked in the way you want it

- Practice your smile one last time

Presenting your speech:

- When you move to the podium/table for your speech, don't tap or blow on the mic.

- Speak into the mic—holding it close enough to make yourself clear and audible.

- Remember, a lot of your audience will give up quickly if they can't hear you

◊ Project your voice to the back row and to those wearing hearing aids

- If you were impressed, and you can tie it in to your speech, you may want to refer to a previous speaker's remarks in a positive way

◊ If they had a quote you liked, referring back to the quote either at the beginning or later in your speech is always a nice touch.

- You're ready to do a great job. Enjoy yourself as much as you can.

Note: In this table, I share tips for preparing a speech for a public engagement.

Audience and Purpose Determine the Word Choice

An important piece in planning your speech is to consider word choice and the background knowledge of your audience. Precise and relatable vocabulary is key to conveying your message—while still being able to connect with the audience.

Two-bit and two-buck words. "May I utilize your automobile?" or "May I use your car?" When we use different forms of English in varying contexts, we codeswitch to ensure we meet the varying needs of our audience and purpose. This is why sometimes we need to use bigger or smaller words; this is what I call two-bit (simpler words) and two-buck words (larger, more complicated words). Two-bit words can act as a lubricant in a speech. These words are familiar and comfortable and allow the listener to let their mental guard down for an instant, while possibly even cracking a smile. Even when speaking to an academic group or teaching a graduate level class, most listeners appreciate when some two-bit words (i.e. everyday words) are sprinkled in with the required two-buck words (i.e. academic vocabulary or content-area vocabulary). Leaders often use the thesaurus to find simpler or fancier word choices when considering the audience. Remember that most newspapers and public texts are written at a 5th-6th grade reading level so the majority of the public can understand the content. For this same reason, speeches should often be written at a simpler level so that most of the audience can understand and relate to your presentation.

Many of us have had the experience of listening to a professor, speaker, or trainer who spoke like their main objective was to impress the audience with their elevated, elite vocabulary. I remember a sociology professor who broke into mind-numbing, sleep-inducing, content-specific vocabulary whenever a student asked a question he didn't know or care to answer. His vocabulary did little to connect with his audience of college students and showed that he hadn't considered his audience. Experiences such as these have motivated me to make a special effort to match my vocabulary and delivery style to the audience. On the other hand, we have likely also experienced times when two-bit vocabulary created a connection with the audience. Years ago, at the conclusion of a rather tense interview with a newspaper reporter about an alleged misconduct incident with one of my staff members, the reporter asked me, "So you believe your staff member's story of what happened last night?" I said, "Yep," and then the interview was over. The next day, "Yep" was on the front page of the local newspaper. Over the next few weeks, people shared how my use of "yep," as compared to "yes," "affirmative," "absolutely," or "indeed," had made the article more believable and relatable.

It takes a combination of expertise, skill, and attitude for a speaker to make the extra effort to adjust their vocabulary and presentation style to the level of their audience. I'm always inspired and appreciative when I can tell a speaker has made that effort. I like the example of the professor who, when speaking to a doctoral level class on plant physiology, used all of the elevated scientific vocabulary needed to engage and cover the material at such a high level. Two hours later, the same person spoke to a high school horticulture class using simpler words to teach how plants worked. And finally, when presenting to his granddaughter's third grade class, he brought straws, sponges, colored water, and a child's vocabulary to teach how plants moved liquids around. The audience, in this case, made all the difference in how the expert presented the material. Leaders can learn from this anecdote because it shows how much the audience should influence the delivery, even if the content is the same.

Acronyms, slang, and lingo: Comprehension stoppers and isolators. Leaders need to consider the importance of scaffolding (gradually increasing the difficulty) of important vocabulary. When introducing necessary concepts to new team members, remind yourself that vocabulary being introduced for the first time should be simple, with definitions and explanations to accompany any new terms, acronyms or lingo. Because of my own experiences with trying to keep up with unfamiliar vocabulary, I have learned even a sprinkling of unknown words can be a comprehension stopper. Because of this, I pay attention to the audience as my presentation or speech progresses— do their faces look confused? or are they nodding in agreement? I work hard to ensure they understand the content of my words, and I need to be willing to reword parts of the presentation with enough two-bit words to regain the audience's understanding before moving on. Don't lose your patience or raise your voice when your audience doesn't understand. Only through patience and scaffolding can a speaker ensure the audience comprehends difficult concepts, especially after using difficult new, or two-buck words. My rule of thumb is—When in doubt, simplify the vocabulary—go two-bit over two-buck every time.

Even focused listeners with positive attitudes toward the speaker and topic, can find slang, lingo, and acronyms to be barriers. However, as was true with our Canadian energy team (see Chapter 6), there may be times when lingo and acronyms are necessary. When this is the case, an effective strategy is to take careful notes on the acronyms the first time you hear them. As you learn more about the meanings of the letters, the context will provide a reminder of the meaning of the acronym. If the speaker doesn't volunteer the meaning of the acronym, don't wait until the end of the talk, raise your hand and ask them right away. Two good things happen with this strategy: (1) the speaker will define the meaning of that acronym within the context of their remarks, and (2) they may remember to clarify the meaning of future acronyms.

Lingo and acronyms are often used in different cultures, professions, and organizations. Though such specialized terms may be comfortable to members of the group, care must be used by any speaker to not let specialized lingo and acronyms stand in the way of their message. Speaking for myself, unfamiliar acronyms and lingo can make me feel like an outsider, even around my own team. I feel embarrassed and uncomfortable when I'm the one that doesn't get the joke because I don't know what's being said.

Though the various English language dialects of Black, Indigenous, and People of Color (BIPOC) are certainly not slang, lingo, or acronyms, dialect can also be conversation and comprehension stoppers. With different dialects spoken in different parts of the United States, until the listener becomes familiar with the pronunciations and meanings of each dialect, leaders will need to make a special effort to quickly learn the nuances of the various Englishes of the audience.

Learning to Speak Clearly in Public

In "The Perils of Not Carefully Preparing Your Speech," readers learn how important it is to prepare carefully for major speeches or presentations. I share the hesitancy, lack of confidence, and panic I sometimes feel when I'm speaking in front of a group. The story "Like Speaking a Foreign Language" shares a personal experience about a time when lingo and acronyms were conversation and comprehension stoppers for my team and me. In both of these stories, the focus is on the importance of choosing the right words at the right time for the right audience.

The Perils of Not Carefully Preparing Your Speech

Early in my career, I didn't spend a significant amount of time preparing to give a speech to any audience. Most of the large group audiences I worked with were at coaching clinics or meetings with parents. As a counselor, I often trained parent groups in guidance topics such as filling out a financial aid form or how to help their child select and apply to the college or university of their choice. In both coaching and counseling, I worked with these topics every day. The subject matter was largely the same year-to-year, and the audience always had a strong attention level because they truly valued the information I was presenting. In short, those speeches were usually fun for me and viewed as worthwhile to my audiences.

But, two experiences in the same year pushed me into a new level of awareness and commitment to carefully preparing for my speeches. It was the middle of December, and I was asked to be the keynote speaker at a combined meeting of several Rotary clubs. It was a noon luncheon, and over 200 people were gathered to hear a 30 minute speech with a slide presentation about a week-long camp I had taken 19 athletes to in Southern Oregon. Because I'd planned to use the slideshow I'd created to guide my narrative, I knew I wouldn't need to prepare notes. The night before, I packed the projector in the car, prepared to give my speech the next day.

After lunch and an introduction by the Rotary president, I took the microphone, made a joking comment about the 20 degree weather outside, and pushed the "on" switch on the projector. I immediately heard a "ping," and the projector light went dark. A guy sitting in the front row asked, "You didn't leave that projector in your car last night, did you? The change in temperature will do that every time." So there I stood, microphone in hand, with no slides, no notes, and no preparation. The audience was totally understanding. I made it through my presentation fairly well, but I'll never forget that empty feeling, and the sound of that "ping." I learned three important lessons: (1) have prepared notes, (2) leave your projector in your house the night before your speech, and (3) always bring an extra bulb.

The second lesson I learned about not preparing for a speech happened two months later. I was on my way to the local community college to attend a parent orientation on the new Financial Aid Form Student Application (FAFSA). The form is similar to an IRS tax form and the numbers, percentages, and calculations change each year. A counselor from the college always led this meeting, reviewing the changes and leading the parents and counselors through completing the form, including answering any questions the audience might have.

I arrived 15 minutes early and was visiting with other counselors in attendance, when the college administrative assistant came into the room. She was carrying a box full of FAFSA forms for the parents and a half inch thick "Counselor's Guide," with overhead transparencies for the presenter. She said, "Harry, Darrell had a family emergency, and he told me to have you handle the orientation tonight." In this case, I wasn't prepared because I wasn't expecting to present that night. To this day, I don't know why the college administrative assistant singled me out to do the presentation—or why I agreed. But, I did learn a lesson that night that I remember to this day—careful preparation and practice are keys to successful public presentations.

When I began to speak, I felt blood rushing to my head. Over 100 parents and 20 counselors were in the room, which suddenly felt like it was 90 degrees. I explained to the audience that I would be leading the orientation and started into the form. It was hard. Even with basic personal information, parents still had at least a few questions. Though I was normally a confident speaker, I felt shaky, and I'm sure the audience could tell. I was not relaxing as the presentation continued, but rather getting more and more stressed. About halfway through the calculations section, a parent asked me a math percentage question, and I froze up. I could feel myself getting dizzy and less able to respond. At that time, a counselor from another school , who I didn't know, spoke up and answered the man's question. I thanked her for helping and invited the rest of the crowd to participate and answer any other questions as we proceeded through the form.

In Table 7.1 at the beginning of this chapter, I shared detailed tips on how to carefully prepare for major speeches. I once heard an adage that applies to preparing speeches. "The harder you work, the luckier you get," or more specifically, "The more carefully you prepare, the smoother and more effective your speech will be."

People have asked me over the years what they could do for stage fright symptoms like I describe in the FASFA story. Some steps I take include: (1) I make sure my sleep bank is solid, (2) I stay away from caffeine before any speech or presentation, and (3) I always keep water nearby during the presentation itself. I often select a breathing technique and practice the technique in non-pressure situations until I get comfortable with it. I now always keep notes handy, even in short speeches. I think the best way to prevent stage fright is through strong preparation using the steps included in this chapter.

Like Speaking a Foreign Language

"Like Speaking a Foreign Language" is a true story that focuses on how acronyms and lingo can halt learning, even with a committed team. The following example happened to my newly formed consulting team the week before we were to leave for Canada (see Chapter 6 for more on this experience). Even though the following story is partly humorous, the sobering fact remained— my team, though experienced and dedicated, was new to energy and much of the time, the oil guys and consultants were speaking a foreign language. We desperately needed to master the information and be able to communicate with the energy team in order to succeed with our upcoming assignment in Canada.

Sixteen people assembled in Spokane for our first meetings, which lasted over the course of one week. Around the table were three representatives of the energy client, four Spokane consultants, five experienced consultants from around the U.S and Canada, and my four man team of educators. This was the same group that my team of leadership experts would be working with over the next three years, with some of the consultants focusing on different contracts with the same client.

After introductions, the consultant who originally earned the opportunity to work with the company began to speak about the contract and the challenges it brought. Having worked the previous several years consulting in energy, he used acronyms from both the energy and the consulting worlds. Between the acronyms and the lingo, the consultants and the energy people may as well have been speaking Russian, and if they knew it, they didn't seem to care. This lesson on language barriers later played a major role in the vocabulary we selected for our on-site training program and written training binder.

After lunch, each of the three groups were to separate and prepare a summary of their roles moving forward. As we worked on our assignment, we joked about how tough it was to keep up because of all the acronyms. Though we normally thought of ourselves as a fairly competent and confident bunch, we quickly agreed not to interrupt and ask for any acronym clarifications in the afternoon. We didn't want to make it that obvious that the acronyms were making us feel out of our league. When we regrouped to share our roles, the energy client team spoke first. They were clearly in a competition to use every acronym known to petroleum and gas. During their presentation, we kept great eye-contact, took notes, smiled, and nodded our heads, but we were already planning our own presentation in our heads. When it came to acronyms, the other consultant team members also outdid themselves. Fortunately, both presentations went over time, and our presentation (aka the Curriculum/Training Team) would kick off the next day's meeting. Much of what could have been three hours of solid learning had been lost due to the lingo and acronyms.

As we drove home that night, our heads reeled with acronyms. For our presentation the next morning, rather than sharing our subject matter as we had previously planned, we decided to go for humor, and to bluntly make our point about how the use of so many acronyms by both groups had made it difficult to follow what they were saying. We included as many of the hundreds of educational acronyms as we could in our presentation. As we drove in the next morning, we laughed as we rehearsed our acronym-laced presentations. And when we started presenting, they didn't have a clue what we were talking about.

Most people in the room quickly figured out what we were doing. They laughed nervously and tried to keep up. Our presentations turned out to be a nice icebreaker, and even a team builder. As the laughs continued over the next two days, we knew we had made our point. During the rest of the week, the others tried to cool it with the acronyms. When they slipped and used one, they stopped themselves and explained the acronyms to everyone. This turned out to be an important lesson about how acronyms and lingo impacted comprehension and created barriers to communication.

Conclusion

Chapter 7 explored leader behaviors that can impact trust bridges with larger audiences. The time and effort to plan and prepare when speaking in public results in less embarrassment and stress for the speaker. The speaker has the power to select just the right vocabulary level and presentation style for their audience. Taking the time to carefully prepare and to adjust those selections builds stronger bridges with audiences of any size. Finally, this chapter confronted the negative impact that lingo and acronyms can have on the speaker's bridge-building efforts. The negative speaker behaviors revealed in this chapter will help guide us all in efforts to build bridges with our teams, our families and our friends.

Readers can use Table 7.2 to apply skills and strategies for speaking to larger audiences. Choosing just the right word and considering the audience's needs is a key to creating stronger bridges of trust.

Table 7.2
Action Plan: Don't say "Utilize

What are two takeaways from this section? 1. 2.
What two strategies will you use to improve your communication with large audiences? 1. 2.
What steps will you take now? (Action Step for Don't Say Utilize)

Note: This table provides readers with a place to review the importance of planning and preparing to get your message across in larger group settings.

CHAPTER 8

TOOL #8: POSITION POWER, THE LESS YOU USE IT, THE GREATER YOUR POWER BECOMES

"Position Power" addresses issues encountered as a leader climbs the professional ladder, moving into positions with more influence and power. The first section of the chapter introduces the concept of a 2 + 2 = 5 team and examines the leader's crucial role in building a successful team. The synergy created by a powerful team can result in the sum equaling more than the individual parts. The second section, The Impacts of Humor on the Team, explores the result of using different types of humor, including inappropriate humor in the workplace. The next section in the chapter dives into the unique challenges of position power, including adjusting to a new leadership position. Most of the strategies and "dos and don'ts" are applicable when taking any new position, but special attention is given to being promoted from within. The final section explores leadership behaviors that can build the trust bridges necessary to result in the leader's personal power becoming stronger than the position power on the team.

The Leader's Role in Building a 2 + 2 = 5 Team

If you go down to the employment office and hire four people who have never met each other to do some work for your business, you've hired a group of four people, not a team. Team relationships don't happen immediately in the workplace; they are built over time as people create trust bridges and relationships. As they work, you may notice that one person has a negative impact on the other three. You now have a 2 + 2 = 3 team. In this situation, the sum of the parts doesn't equal the whole - one of the employees is impacting the rest of the team's success. In fact, leaders might notice that when a certain teammate stays home that day, the team gets more done. When leaders learn of these 2 + 2 = 3 situations, they must be ready to take on the tough conversations that will make the team whole (see "SIDWI" in Chapter 1 or "Don't Wake a Sleeping Doberman" in Chapter 5). If the group of four creates a synergy that causes them to accomplish more than anticipated, they become a 2 + 2 = 5 team. They are better together than individually, and each team member complements the skills of the others. Most of us have been part of both types of teams in the past. But, leaders want their teams to evolve into a 2 + 2 = 5 team.

There are several core traits that exemplify a 2 + 2 = 5 team: trust, respect, communication, planning, focus, predictability, and training (see Table 8.1). In the following section, I share descriptions for each of these traits. Direct results and by-products of the long-term presence of the 2 + 2 = 5 ingredients often include a team that cares for each other, both on and off the job. There is usually appropriate humor and good will at the jobsite. Smiles and laughter permeate the environment and often lead to a sense of joy, both at work and at home. Feelings of pride and satisfaction for a job well done also lead to less stress, high attendance at work, and less turnover.

Table 8.1
Traits of a 2 + 2 = 5 team

1.	Trust—both ways, all for one and one for all approach
2.	Respect—patient, positive and supportive team talk
3.	Communication—up, down and across the system, no surprises
4.	Planning—detailed road map to success, timelines, benchmarks
5.	Clear focus on team goals and expectations
6.	Predictability—no surprises
7.	Strong, specific training and opportunities for professional development

Note: This table includes the main traits that should be exhibited to establish and sustain a 2 + 2 = 5 team.

Trust

The predominant trait in 2 + 2 = 5 teams is a bond of trust between the teammates, along with a two-way trust bridge with the leader. Knowing they can count on one another and the leader to show up on time and work hard every day, the team begins to add Elmer's glue to their bridge. Though they may not be close, personal friends outside of work, the team's trust bridges become strong.

Mutual Respect

Another key building block for a 2 + 2 = 5 team is mutual respect. When the leader models respect with team members, they are empowered to show respect to the leader, as well as to their teammates. A common manifestation of respect is patience. Patience for differing personalities and beliefs allows team members and the leader to relax and focus on the task at hand. With mutual respect in place, teammates begin to put the needs of the team above their own needs, and this type of trust and respect on a team results in a "one for all, all for one" mentality. They understand and are committed to building and sustaining the synergy for their team to succeed.

Communication

Still another factor in building a strong team is a commitment to clear communication up, down, and sideways on the chain of command. Strong communication is a key to building and sustaining synergy. $2 + 2 = 5$ teammates that trust and respect each other often engage in positive and supportive talk. Such positive talk leads to increased feelings of value and appreciation for each member's strengths. The leader can also contribute to a positive communication environment on the team by modeling the leadership filter and by demonstrating respect when disciplining or talking with team members one-on-one (see "Leadership Filter" in Chapter 3, specifically Figure 3.2 and Table 3.2, and tips for one-on-one conversations in Chapters 1 & 4).

Planning

The traits of trust, respect, and communication are cornerstones of a $2 + 2 = 5$ team. However, many of us may have been on teams where these three traits were strengths, yet the team was limited in its ability to reach its goals because of poor planning. Not only can poor planning lead to slower progress toward team goals, it can also lead to frustration, conflict, and loss of confidence and morale, even by a talented team. The phases of a quality planning process include team input and detailed, visible, and frequent communication (see Table 8.2).

Table 8.2
Planning for a 2 + 2 = 5 Team

Steps that will help in planning for a successful 2 + 2 = 5 team include:
• Gathering team input on all aspects of the proposed project   ◊ This provides quality information, as well as a feeling of ownership by the team members
• Detailed communication and positive energy at the introduction of the plan
• Visible and frequent communication about how the project timeline is progressing, including frequent digital communication and department updates
• A visible, detailed project timeline, with benchmarks and dates can be displayed throughout the project work areas, as a visual reminder and conversation source among team members.
• Adapting plans to respond to changes that impact the team
• Celebrating small and large wins as they move along the project plan timeline.

Note: This table provides some tips for planning that incorporate trust building strategies.

Focus

Successful 2 + 2 = 5 teams are known for their clear focus on team goals. When following the team plan and timelines, team members know exactly how they fit into the overall team objectives, and they grow to understand why their daily work is vital to reaching team and company goals. Maintaining a strong focus can be a major role for mid-managers and department leaders. Many of the positive, bridge-building skills explored in *The Ten Tools* can contribute to the leader's success in maintaining the strong focus on goals by all team members.

Predictability

Along with employing a predictable timeline and detailed plan, 2 + 2 = 5 teams believe in the doctrine of no surprises. Surprises, such as sudden and unexpected changes in a plan, can derail even strong teams. The larger the impact of the unexpected change, the more pronounced the team response will be. Unanticipated changes not only disrupt the person affected, such surprises also impact the morale and the productivity of the entire team. The long-term and domino effect can compromise the credibility of the leader, as well as the positive momentum the team had before the change.

Training

Up-to-date and specific training is an irreplaceable component of any 2 + 2 = 5 team, and because of the pride they take in individual and team excellence, 2 + 2 = 5 teams expect to be thoroughly trained. Realizing that a person can't be expected to perform at a higher level unless they've been trained to that higher level, leadership needs to allocate resources to keep quality training available for their teams. Such quality training will improve the work environment and rapidly strengthen the team's overall performance. People who know they are well-trained feel competent and confident, and their confidence allows them to experience less stress and focus directly on team goals. Well-trained teammates are often able to complete their own tasks, while reaching out to add support to the overall team effort.

2 + 2 = 5 Teams Enjoy Humor

Appropriate humor on a regular basis can benefit a team in a number of ways. When you poke fun at yourself, it can be endearing to the team. Showing a sense of humor can also cause the team to relax and focus on their jobs. The positive body chemicals released by humor and laughter benefit everyone on the team. Appropriate workplace jokes can be used as icebreakers to start a meeting and/or to end a staff meeting on a positive note.

Inappropriate humor can damage a 2 + 2 = 5 team. As we learned in kindergarten, "It's not funny unless it's funny to everyone." There is never a right time for inappropriate humor in the workplace. Focus on the side of safety. If the humor is even close to being inappropriate, leave it out. If a teammate starts to tell an inappropriate story or joke, stop them immediately: "Jerry, please, let's not go there." If Jerry continues, use a larger hammer approach—remembering that you, as the leader, are accountable for any potential violation of safe workplace or sexual harassment standards. Step toward Jerry and say, "I said no, Jerry. This is not an appropriate place for that joke/story." If Jerry continues, say, "Jerry, leave the room now." If Jerry refuses to leave and tries to continue the joke, adjourn the meeting and excuse everyone from the room. Your role is to protect the rest of your team from the inappropriate comments.

Strategies for Building a 2 + 2 = 5 Team

Leaders who want to build and lead 2 + 2 = 5 teams should be purposeful with strategies that build trust bridges and strength within their teams. Some specific trust building strategies are included below (see Table 8.3)

Table 8.3
Trust Building Blocks

---

1. Team Information Sheet (see Figure 8.4)

---

2. Schedule times for trust building activities on your calendar.

These activities include:

- Meet regularly with team (hand out a written agenda)

    ◊ Be early, greet teammates at the door (encourages punctuality)

    ◊ Touch base, read body language, stay on top of team dynamics

    ◊ Recognize team, or family accomplishments

    ◊ Remind of upcoming events or deadlines

    ◊ Bring munchies

- Meet with team members one-on-one

    ◊ Builds trust bridges, respect, caring, common experiences

    ◊ Stay up to speed on what's going on in their lives

        ▪ Send a quick note to respond to joy and sadness in their lives

- Be visible in their work space

    ◊ Make it a regular event, not an occasional surprise

    ◊ Share a quick thank you afterward

        ▪ Written notes, including texts and emails allow them to refer back to the note and/or share with others

    ◊ Check off names to make sure you're getting to everybody

---

Note. This table lists ways to connect with your team to build trust.

Team Information Sheet

A top strategy for building community among the team is creating a "Team Information Sheet" (see Table 8.4). This sheet includes contact information, such as the team member's first and last name, home mailing address, and cell phone number, as well as connecting information, like the name of their spouse/significant other/partner; names and ages of their children; their high school name, graduation year and number of students in their senior class; their college alma mater(s); and birthday month and day. This sheet is optional for team members, and they can omit specific information if they wish, but most teammates like the idea and join in. Each team member receives a copy of the information sheet, but because there is a need to maintain confidentiality and make sure nobody's privacy is compromised, this connecting sheet should be solely for the use of the team and should never be shared electronically to ensure only those on the team have access.

Table 8.4
Sample Team Information Sheet

	Team Roster						
Team Member Name and Position	Spouse	Children, (names and ages)	High school (name, graduation year, number of students in graduating class)	College(s) (name, degree, graduation year)	Home Address	Phone #s	Birth date (month and year)
Harry Amend, Superintendent	•	• • •	• • •	• •	•	•	•

Note: This table can be adjusted to include any other information that the team or team leader deems necessary. The main purpose of this information is to create a space for team members to connect on a personal level and learn more about each other.

This sheet provides each person on the team information about the rest of the team that could help create stronger relationships. For example, discovering that another person attended high school or college at the same school or finding out another teammate has kids the same age might be a way for teammates to forge connections.

Building Time for Trust

Building trust is a key component in building and sustaining a $2 + 2 = 5$ team, and spending quality time with the team is one way for leaders to build and maintain that vital trust. There is often a punch list needing to be accomplished in the day or week. Leaders often gravitate toward tangible, measurable, time-driven items like completing a report, delivering a message, or finishing up a project. Checking the item off the list and moving on to the next, quantifiable and tangible item is gratifying, but as experienced leaders, we should know better. Leaders need to be disciplined at carving out time from the daily hourglass to schedule trust building meetings with team members. Those meetings should be near the top of the to-do list. Using the strategies listed in Table 8.3, you can build trust by creating time slots on your calendar for team meetings, one-on-one meetings, and roam times.

Regular informal group meetings. Meeting regularly with the team with at least a brief agenda is important. Informal meetings give leaders a chance to read body language and stay in the loop on team dynamics. These meetings create an opportunity to recognize team or family accomplishments and to remind the team of upcoming events or deadlines. Make sure there are munchies such as baked goods, fruit, veggies, nuts, or a meat and cheese tray. Even in these days of gluten-free, vegans, and vegetarians, the team will appreciate the thought, and there will rarely be any donuts left by the end of the day.

One-on-one meetings. Positive one-on-one meetings can be powerful for building trust bridges between a leader and a teammate. The lack of other distractions allows the leader to focus solely on the other person. Eye contact, nodding, and positive word choices in these one-on-one meetings can provide a sense of safety that promotes openness and honesty. Many people share that a one-on-one conversation with their boss thawed a strained relationship and/or started a positive, long-term relationship.

Visibility. Walk throughs show the team the leader wants to connect with what they're doing. There is something about the boss being visible in the hallways and workspace that is endearing. Stopping by to observe and give them a smile or thumbs-up communicates that they are important to their leader and to the team.

Sometimes leaders get so focused on managing marginal employees, they forget to experience the joy of spending time with the superstars. Spread the benefits of an attentive and caring boss to every employee on the team. Use a physical checklist of the team to record the dates when informal contact was made with each employee to ensure that you spend equal amounts with each team member. Without the checkmark, you may unconsciously gravitate toward particular team members.

Personal attention motivates each teammate in an individualized way. Some team members may prefer talking about non-school topics if given the choice. If the leader discovers interests that are important to the teammate, the conversation can provide an enjoyable break in the workday routine for both the teammate and the leader. When people share their passion about the team and work, walls come down and trust grows. Like a great teacher, you learn to individualize the care of your team members as you learn each person's strengths and play to those strengths as their leader. For instance, you will learn how each person prefers to be praised or recognized (i.e. publicly or privately, verbally or in writing). You learn whether the person responds better to a more formal vocabulary and demeanor or if they prefer a more casual approach. You learn whether they enjoy being asked about their family or prefer to keep it professional.

A smile, nod, thumbs up, quick conversation, or positive question are all strong bridge-building connectors leaders can use to follow-up on a walk through. A handwritten note (including the date) should always be sent out afterward. These notes might include messages such as, "Thanks for letting me drop by today and watch...," "It was cool seeing how your students responded to...," or "You were doing a great job..." Notice that these responses include detailed, specific praise for what the leader observed that day.

Handwritten notes, smiles, thumbs-up, and the various responses described in this section will all bring a smile to any team member. The affirmation that team members receive for doing their jobs on a daily basis can help to build trust bridges and 2 + 2 = 5 teams.

Position Power in New Leadership Roles

Position power refers to the direct influence a person has over a team or situation based on a title or a specific assignment. Position power does not rely on personal relationships between the leader and the followers. It is the title, assigned by a higher authority, that provides the influence necessary for the leader to get their job done. Position power can be assigned for long and short periods of time. Position power is common in the military setting, where respect is often expected based on rank, rather than on the person's ability or character.

The goal of any new leader should be to gain the respect of the team through character, knowledge, and ability, rather than through the title. A promotion may get leaders into a bigger office, but only positive relationships with the team keeps them there. The less you use the new title and its position power as leverage, the more realized power you create with your team. The power for leading the team grows from competence, expertise, and building and sustaining trust bridges with new team members. Over time, these individual and team bridges lead to personal and professional bonds, resulting in a 2 + 2 = 5 team.

Personal Power Becomes Stronger Than Position Power

Personal power is based on such personal attributes as integrity, compassion, and honesty. Personal power can be gained by demonstrating the characteristics of being a patient listener, a strong decision maker, a good planner, or a strong advocate for the team. As the leader displays these personal attributes and tools, the trust bridge is gradually built. Over time, the team begins to transfer power to the leader because of these qualities, rather than the title. Several leadership traits that transform position power to personal power for team leaders are included below (see Table 8.5).

Table 8.5
Leader Traits that Transfer Position Power to Personal Power

1.	Become a great listener, carve out the time, and use SIDWI skills ◊ Affirm the person, ◊ Care about and respect them ◊ Earn their trust
2.	Display integrity, compassion, and honesty
3.	Earn the reputation of honoring confidentiality
4.	Use team input to make decisions
5.	Show the courage and skills to have challenging one-one-one conversations with people
6.	Explain clearly when relaying information ◊ Explain without complaining, casting a negative vibe, or blaming someone else
7.	Earn the level of trust that will cause the team to speak the truth, even if they think it may upset the leader

Note: This table lists behaviors that build the credibility of a leader and enhance the transfer of position power to personal power.

Taking the time to sincerely listen is a clear sign that the leader cares about and respects the team. During conversations with team members, listening carefully can earn trust in several ways. For example, when the leader uses ideas shared during conversations with team members to make decisions for the team, it demonstrates confidence in the team member in a tangible way that encourages them to continue sharing ideas and innovations with the leader. Additionally, when the leader learns something confidential about a team member, ensuring that person's confidentiality builds trust. People feel more comfortable turning to the leader to share private information once the leader's reputation for compassion and integrity is established. As mentioned previously, having tough conversations with team members is a bridge-builder that enhances the leader's personal power (see Chapter 4 & 5 for more information on having tough one-on-one conversations). When the team sees the leader address the 5% rather than the entire team, this demonstrates the leader's thoughtfulness and purposefulness (see Chapter 4).

A key outcome of strong trust between team members and the leader is the willingness of the team to speak the truth. When key decisions may be controversial, leaders need accurate information in order to make the best decisions for all stakeholders. Three strategies to getting accurate information from the team are: (1) Always be clear about why the information is needed and why it is best for the team for the leader to have the truth; (2) Encourage and remind the team that it takes courage to tell the truth and why the truth is necessary even when the leader may not be happy; and (3) Use positive body language and sincerity when hearing good and bad information. Even if the information is upsetting, leaders need to try to control their own emotions and minimize any negative facial expression and body language. The goal is to assure the team that it is safe to bring information to the top.

One reality of leadership is that there will be times when you don't have control over a situation. The words and actions may come as directives from leaders up the hierarchy. You must serve as the messenger during these situations, and your words and body language should not portray a negative twist to the message. Supporting the team over the wishes of the boss will not cause trust or loyalty with the team at the school or job site; rather, this sort of action demonstrates disloyalty to the entire organization, and team members may lose trust. Being a team player applies to the leader, too, and people will understand and respect hearing messages without a negative spin or opinion. Also, blaming the boss and/or expressing disagreement or regret over a decision will certainly be relayed back up the chain, which could damage trust bridges between you and your boss.

Balancing New Position Power: Promoted from Within

Being promoted from within can be one of the most rewarding and challenging experiences that can happen during a leader's career. Former colleagues may have mixed feelings, wishing the upper leadership had hired an outsider or feeling relieved to have a leader who already "knows the team." Building trust bridges in this new context will take time and patience. Some former colleagues will be eager to build or modify bridges, while others may be hesitant, or even unwilling, to do so. Becoming familiar with each teammate's response enables you to develop an individualized approach and sense of timing that matches each person's desires and needs. Allowing flow time as teammates settle in and adjust emotionally to this new professional relationship builds credibility, confidence, and trust.

New leaders that are promoted from within should adhere to the following cautions: (1) Don't come in too hot, (2) Don't mention upper leadership, (3) Don't bad-mouth your predecessor, (4) Don't assume you know the politics, and (5) Don't overpromise (see Table 8.6). These tips will help new leaders to navigate those early days, weeks, and months in a position where the faculty and staff already know them.

Table 8.6
Cautions When Being Promoted from Within

1. Don't Come in Too Hot— watch your body language, as well as your words

   ◊ "There's a new sheriff in town"

   ◊ "I've already been told everything about you guys"

2. Don't lean on, or frequently mention those who promoted you

   ◊ Your team may already have differing opinions about those people

      ▪ This could cause your team to look at you, and see that other person

   ◊ Show your team you're looking forward, not backward

3. Don't bad-mouth your predecessor

   ◊ Their supporters are still on the team, possibly in the room

4. Don't assume the team hierarchy will stay the same

   ◊ Different personalities may rise to the fore if they mesh better with you

   ◊ Former team leaders may gladly, or begrudgingly take a lesser role

5. Don't over promise

   ◊ Control your wishful thinking

   ◊ Betting on hope that doesn't come to fruition can damage credibility

Note: This table lists key behaviors to avoid when being promoted to a new job within your organization.

Two dynamics often exist when a new leader arrives. One dynamic is that new leaders want to appear as knowledgeable as possible to their new team. Even leaders who have been promoted from within want, and need, to establish credibility in their new role. Former co-workers may already have an opinion on the new leader's integrity, personality, and work ethic, but they will now be assessing the new leader's skill set in the new position. The leader should study any available written information about the team, in addition to gathering information from other people, such as board members, staff members, stakeholders, and friends. The other dynamic is the team's belief in their own uniqueness. They believe that you cannot really know the most important things about them until you have worked with them. The new leader needs to honor team feelings and use words and body language carefully. Make sure not to communicate feelings like, "There's a new sheriff in town" or " I already know everything about your team."

You need to be careful not to lean on those who placed you in your new position or rely solely on the position power of your new title. If you do, some team members could question your competence and resent the forced nature of your position power. It will be up to you to look forward and focus on building the trust bridges to succeed as their leader.

Leaders should remember that some of their predecessor's supporters are still on the team, and may even be in the room. Bad-mouthing a predecessor is a sensitive dynamic. A brief statement that recognizes and speaks positively of the predecessor can take the possible negative emotional edge off the team. For example, "I know many of you are close to Sue, and I want you to know that I think highly of her as well." By making this type of brief statement, the new leader honors feelings that may be present in some of their new team, in addition to honoring the predecessor.

Don't assume the previous team's political hierarchy will stay the same under new leadership. The new leader needs to remember that different team personalities will rise to the fore while others will take a lesser role based on relationships with the new leader. The leader needs to reassure any team members that may feel less important while making a point to encourage new leaders evolving on the team. The goal is to create and maintain as many positive leadership behaviors as possible on the new team.

A final mistake that new leaders need to guard against is overpromising. The leader may feel that every positive idea should be mentioned and focused on at the very beginning of their tenure, but wishful thinking and hope that does not come to fruition right away—or ever—could lead to disappointment and a loss of credibility. The adage of underpromise and overdeliver is a good strategy for starting out a relationship with a team.

Using Strategies to Create Strong Teams

To support the tools shared in Chapter 8, I've chosen two important stories. First, I share a story to illustrate how to create and sustain a 2 + 2 = 5 team relationship. The story shares the experience of a young team that toiled long and hard, both physically and emotionally toward a lofty, seemingly impossible goal. "Lesson Learned from a Grandma at the Water Fountain" is a story from the high plains of Montana that illustrates how difficult, and important, it is for a leader to get accurate information when making decisions.

The Lions: A 2 + 2 = 5 Team Born Out of Necessity

In the town where the Lions lived, there were 20 baseball teams for players aged 12 and under. But once kids turned 13, there were only 10 teams, which meant there were only half as many spots available for kids to play. There were a lot of disappointed 13-year olds who didn't make the cut for a spot on the 10 available teams in the 13 and under league.

Recognizing a need to create additional opportunities for players who didn't have a spot on the current teams, a call went out to create a new team. Thirteen players and families responded, and the Lions became the 11th team in the league. All 13 families were grateful that their son's baseball experience didn't end that year, and everyone was pleased that there would be no out of pocket cost to play for the Lions. Instead, there would be team fundraisers to raise money for uniforms and out of town trips. The only promise made to the parents was that their son would improve as a player and teammate and would experience the joy of playing baseball.

The Lions practiced in a large, indoor shop owned by one of the families on Sunday evenings beginning in September. As each player and parent came into the shop the first few times, there was shyness and nervousness. As the parents watched from a balcony area, the three coaches made sure the players worked hard for two hours every Sunday. They were exhausted at the end of each practice. The parents and players had all been told, in writing, that Sunday practices were optional. With the help of a lot of carpooling and an occasional overnight stay, from September through the start of the season in April, there was virtually 100% attendance at Sunday practices.

At the first parent/player meeting, the following goals were made clear:

- Every player would learn to play at least two positions.

- All 13 players would learn to pitch, including at least one off-speed pitch.

- Each player was expected to work hard at practice to improve individual and team skills.

- Each player would learn the information in the 35-page Lion's Binder, including all of the offensive and defensive plays the team would be using.

- Every family would participate in the two fundraisers, selling boxes of oranges and grapefruit for the holidays and selling frozen pizzas around Valentines Day.

In the early stages, the parents and players were not a team; they were all individuals on the same team. But, working hard together toward the same goals quickly began to build trust among the young players and the parents. As physical skills improved, mutual respect grew between all 13 players.

Laughter and joy replaced shyness and nervousness. In February, the team had an overnight, team building retreat, which focused on the mental parts of the game covered in their binders. The shared experience of very hard work and focus on common goals created a strong synergy that is present in every 2 + 2 = 5 team.

The team and parents decided to do a community service project and restore the varsity field at the middle school, which was the Lion's home field during the season. When relatives and friends of the team arrived with pickup trucks, four wheelers, edgers, power rakes, and mowers, the Lion army finished the baseball field quickly and moved across the school property and restored the two middle school softball fields, as well. The middle school administrators and coaches were flabbergasted and grateful when they saw the results of the project.

Amazing things happened during the Lion's season. Going into the final tournament, the Lions had a record of 16 wins and 19 losses. In the title game, the Lions came from behind to beat a team they had lost to previously. They won the tournament, and ended the season with a 19-19 record, a team celebration pile on the pitcher's mound, a large trophy, and City Championship shirts. Two years later, 11 out of the 13 Lions were on high school baseball rosters at several high schools. By the spring of 2021, four Lions were on college baseball rosters.

The power and lasting benefits of the Lion's successful 2 + 2 = 5 team created confident young men who continue to use skills and team strategies on different teams and new situations. In this same way, team members and leaders who have 2+2=5 experiences strive to recreate those experiences in future jobs and teams.

A Lesson Learned from a Grandma at the Water Fountain

In this chapter, I described the importance of receiving accurate information and shared strategies for building trust bridges that encourage a person to be willing to speak the truth, even if it may hurt feelings or cause anger.

During my leadership career, false information has thwarted some of my attempts to solve problems. I wasted valuable time and struggled to find a solution due to false facts. By the time I learned that my information was wrong, I made mistakes and damaged trust and relationships. From these experiences, I learned to take my time, to ask extra questions, and to gather as much information as possible before making decisions. My experience in the following story shares a lesson about what happens when you take the time to ask that extra question when searching for the truth.

I was on the trail of a pitching prospect in a tiny town in Northeastern Montana. It had been a hot, dusty day and the mosquitoes were just beginning to come out. I was running late and had already folded up my chair, headed for the car when a tall, lanky, long armed kid came out of the bullpen to pitch. The catcher's glove sounded like a shotgun when he caught the kid's pitches, so I decided to stay and watch another inning.

I could tell the kid had some nice physical tools, but I didn't know anything about his makeup (i.e. mindset or character, including things like mental and emotional stability, work habits, and coachability). How players handle adversity is always a huge factor scouts must consider. Only one out of every 20 players that signs a professional baseball contract ever plays a day in the major leagues, and over half of the players that are signed are released for makeup reasons. Discovering makeup issues is even more important (and difficult) today, when a lot of scouting is conducted via video cameras and radar speed guns—neither of which provide the scout information about the person's makeup.

I saw the kid's family come to life in the bleachers when he stepped onto the pitcher's mound, so I walked over. Both the mom and dad said their son was having a "great year," and they gave me a 100% glowing report on his makeup. As they talked, I saw the boy's grandma, sitting further down the bleachers look down and shake her head. She grabbed her walker and headed over to the water fountain. After saying goodbye to the parents, I walked over to the water fountain. I asked grandma the same questions. She said something like,

"Well, he started to go downhill after he got Susie pregnant. I just don't understand kids nowadays. At least they've decided to keep the baby, and they're getting married right after the season. By the way, you didn't see him at his best just now. He should have started this game, but he got kicked out of last night's game for arguing with the umpire. His elbow surgery hasn't responded that well either, and the doctors say he might have to get the surgery redone. It's been a tough year, but we're still proud of him."

I could have hugged that grandma. In less than two minutes, she had given me all the information I needed to accurately fill out the make-up section of my scouting report.

As I started my three hour drive back toward the motel, I was thankful I'd stopped by that water fountain. I was reminded how important it was to get accurate information before making any decision. The parent's glowing description of how the pitcher's year had gone reminded me of how people could slant their input to favor their own interests, leaving out vital information. Taking the time to double check can make all the difference.

Conclusion

Of the traits explored for creating and sustaining a 2 + 2 = 5 team, the most important factor is trust. The trust between teammates and their leader builds the bridges toward the team's success. Leaders need to commit the time necessary to use strategies, such as those shared in this chapter to build and sustain trust bridges. New leaders need to remember that though a new title gets them into the office, only trust and relationships will create a 2 + 2 = 5 team.

In the action plan for this chapter, readers should consider the most important takeaways from this chapter, and how they can use this new knowledge to improve communication and build strong, 2 + 2 = 5 teams. Each of the examples I shared demonstrate how important it is to take time to develop trust with and get accurate information from teammates. Consider these stories as you create this chapter's action plan (see Table 8.7). Remember to consider specific traits and steps that can build stronger trust and synergy.

Table 8.7
Action Plan: Position Power

What are two takeaways from this section? 1. 2.
What two strategies will you use to improve your Position Power? 1. 2.
What steps will you take now? (Action Step for Position Power)

Note: This table provides readers a chance to review how to build a 2 + 2 = 5 team.

CHAPTER 9

TOOL #9: ADDRESSING THE NEGATIVE IMPACTS OF STRESS ON THE TEAM

This chapter addresses the profound impact that stress can have on teams– both on the jobsite and in their personal lives. There are many different types of emotional challenges a leader faces when leading their team. Leaders cannot prepare in advance to lead in cases of severe emotional stress and trauma caused by unexpected tragedies, and this chapter provides strategies for leaders who find themselves in situations where they are unprepared. Even in tough times, leaders must maintain composure and help their team through the next days, weeks, and months. Leading in times of trauma can cause both short and long-term stress for any leader, but specific approaches can help leaders lead their team through these stressful times.

By practicing some of the tools described in previous chapters (i.e. building trust bridges, making time for relationships with team members, recognizing team members' strengths), leaders can implement these strategies and identify team members that can help during traumatic events. This chapter builds on tools described in Chapters 1-8 by spelling out specific actions to address major challenges, such as the trauma of a sudden event. Leaders can lean on their trust bridges in the workplace and, by using specific actions and words, strengthen relationships.

Leading in Times of Trauma

Within this book, we've explored strategies that improve your effectiveness in communicating with individuals one-on-one and with larger groups. In every case, the importance of assessing and responding to emotions has been emphasized. To review—your body language, tone of voice, pace, and volume are key factors in managing emotions. In previous chapters, the leader has been able to prepare and rehearse the response. Personal or position power determined, or at least influenced, the outcome of the issues being experienced. Because the leader was able to control the conversation, create flow time, and decide which hammer to use, the situations usually resolved favorably. But, leading in times of trauma often leaves the leader powerless to control the outcome of the situation; the best results come from managing the emotional responses that result from the out-of-control circumstances.

Despite my own counseling experience, multiple training sessions, and on-the-job experience, when I received a 4 AM phone call, heard the school lockdown alarm, or saw a law enforcement officer at my office door, I often struggled to push my own emotions aside so that I could lead. Leading families, staff, and communities during traumatic events like violent acts or tragedies does not allow for in-depth planning time for a response, and it does not allow for a leader to get caught up with emotions. The team and community will be looking to the leader for guidance and strength, and the best leaders rise to the occasion.

It's your job to provide detailed, accurate information about an important event as soon as possible. For the public relations department, timely and accurate information at this time is necessary. When you are faced with a tragedy, such as a suicide, death, or traumatic event, here is some guidance for your speech, along with the hope you will never have to use these suggestions. The table that follows provides some specific tips that leaders can use when faced with the unimaginable (see Table 9.1).

Table 9.1
Preparing to Lead When Trauma Hits Your Team

When faced with a traumatic situation, leaders can use the following tips:

1. Take time to prepare. Even if people are waiting for a statement or guidance, take a few moments to write down the key points you need to address. Having notes prepared will help focus the conversation, and reporters, on-site observers, and people receiving information electronically are all accustomed to waiting for the speaker(s).

2. Use pronouns like "we" and "our" to remind the audience that you are part of a team, and you are experiencing the same stress and trauma they are.

3. Don't say things like, "It looks like"..." or, " I think…" Make the extra effort to get the facts straight. In these situations, your conjectures and opinions could be incorrect or could cause the audience more stress. Stick to the facts, be sure to pause frequently, take time to look at your notes, and keep breathing deeply. Reading or speaking slowly allows people to process.

4. As factual information allows, communicate it in writing. Written facts help squash rumors, as well as provide people with flow time to understand and process emotions in their own grief cycle.

5. If people have questions, respond briefly and do not engage with any conjecture. You may not have all the answers, so prepare to say, "I don't have an answer for that right now, but I'll relay the information when I receive it." Use words like, "We haven't heard that." If you hear a rumor you know is false, say, "That is not our understanding."

6. Speaking in a strong, slow, measured voice will help you manage your own emotions and have a calming effect on the audience. Using a calm and confident approach helps the team and stakeholders to follow suit. Make eye contact and keep a neutral face. Even in the saddest of situations, showing patience, understanding, and caring sends a message of stability that can calm emotions.

7. When speaking to a large group of people, whether live, on camera, or recorded, be sure to hold the microphone close to your mouth, so people can hear you clearly. If the microphone needs to be moved away from your mouth slightly, they will let you know.

8. Try to control your own emotions, but when you need to cry, step back from the podium and cry. Your voice may crack when you resume talking, but it will level out.

9. Take a step back. When speaking to your team, stand back far enough from the front row to provide some space. This sense of separation can establish a sense of power and control, which the team will respect.

Note: This table can be used to help leaders who are faced with traumatic situations.

A skilled leader, using many of the skills in *The Ten Tools,* can substantially impact the stress level if they have the courage to step into tough bridge-building conversations. The intensity of supervisor and employee relationships comes from the clear power of daily contact that can be used to hurt or to heal. As leaders learn and use the bridge-building tools of trust and caring, teammates will become healthier and teams will be more successful. Over time, the energy of the team can be focused on team success, not on coping with fear and the resulting debilitating stress.

Managing "Weather Systems"

The term "weather system" is a way of describing the overall mood that permeates a team, job site, or other setting at a given time. You will need to guide your team through all types of weather systems. There will be warm, sunny days when things are going well, the energy is positive, and life is good for the team. There will also be days when life is cloudy and bumpy. Stormy weather could be caused by a traumatic event that impacts the entire team.

Sunny weather. Your team will experience times of joy and celebration. Engagements, weddings, births, graduations, promotions, and great health, family, or team news can all produce strong, positive emotional ties among the team. When these events occur, your team experiences sunny weather. Of course, small situations can also produce happiness and great weather on your team. For instance, teaching a successful lesson plan, making a breakthrough with a difficult student, or even solving a departmental problem can all produce joy for individual staff members. The positive attitude felt by these colleagues can create a productive synergy that spreads to several staff members—or even the entire team. Bonds of love, respect, and friendship created during sunny weather will strengthen your team, and trust bridges built from sharing positive emotional experiences can be strong and enduring. A jobsite where sharing, supporting, and celebrating are part of the culture is a great place to come to work. It will be a culture of commitment, growth, and success.

Positive relationships with teammates can spread and sustain the joy that occurs during sunny weather. Such positive times are a great opportunity for building and strengthening trust bridges between team members and with their leaders. A leader's connection with the team, based on trust, respect and careful observation, can be a major plus in driving team culture. Taking time to pause and celebrate can expand positive energy and create memorable feelings that can help sustain the team when tougher times occur. Other connections such as walkthroughs, one-on-one conversations, and group check-ins (see Chapter 8) also produce sunny weather, while allowing the leader to keep a close emotional watch on every member of their team.

Stormy weather. Sometimes individual ordeals impact the weather system for other members of the team. At other times, community events and larger traumatic issues cause stormy weather. In the following table, I share some strategies for weathering storms (see Table 9.2).

Table 9.2
Leadership Tools for Stormy Weather

1. Be visible and physically present. This increases calm and the feeling of safety. Walking around, visiting with small groups or individuals and listening, with patience and caring, is a powerful leadership behavior in times of trauma and healing.

2. Manage emotions while keeping a clear focus on the jobs that need to be done.

3. Get permission to share information with team and higher administration

4. Help family members and friends dealing with guilt from suicide

   ◊ Dual factors of sadness and guilt are much tougher to process on grief cycle

   ◊ Requires more leader patience

5. Have a trained trauma therapy professional facilitate group grieving sessions with students, staff, and community

6. Have as many trained mental health professionals as possible in the building/worksite until the demand decreases

   ◊ Many will volunteer or be paid by their employer

   ◊ Check for grant funding to cover expenses

7. Depend on your team's intervention strategies

   ◊ Soft skills

   ◊ Connecting one-on-one

   ◊ Empowering team members

8. Be flexible with schedules and procedures to adapt to individual counseling needs

   ◊ Have substitute staff available for flexibility

9. Therapy dogs have a strong calming effect on many people

10. Add virtual communications and instruction during disconnected times like COVID-19 and prolonged weather or natural disaster disruptions

11. When violent events are televised and online perpetually, ask students and staff to not show the events on their devices while at school or work.

   ◊ Repeated exposure to violence causes secondary trauma, especially to children

Note: This table shares some specific strategies for leaders to refer to when dealing directly with a traumatic situation that has caused stormy weather on their team.

I remember a traumatic event that impacted an individual team member and caused cloudy weather for the entire team. It occurred the day Sue came to work after learning her husband had a growth the doctors feared was malignant. Normally a positive and upbeat member of the team, Sue was quiet, weepy, and sobbing. Seeing Sue upset caused several other team members to get stressed out; they wanted to help Sue, and they were also worried about her husband's diagnosis. Since the team still faced a full schedule of work, it was up to me to manage emotions while keeping a clear focus on the jobs that needed to be done. While several teammates and I consoled Sue, I asked for her permission to explain her husband's situation to the team and to the district office. This step helped other team members, who didn't know why Sue was so upset, to understand and get their own emotions under control.

Personal and emotional team issues can bring out the best and the worst in people. A teammate who is usually quiet and on the outside of most team interactions may stand the tallest in being sensitive to another's emotions. Teammates who misunderstood this person, find out they have the instincts, strengths, willingness, and skills to approach the toughest emotional situations. One of your jobs as their leader is to value this from team members. Over time, people with crucial soft skills, empowered to step in and help, may be more valuable to team success than the most successful practitioners. These people can be the silent heroes by adding the glue to hold the bridges together.

If a fellow teammate, such as the person described in the previous paragraph, is not able to make progress with soothing the emotions of a suffering person, another teammate should immediately contact the employee at their jobsite responsible for responding to a medical emergency. When your entire team is trained in this connecting process, this uniform approach of caring enough to ask a hurting teammate, "How are you doing?" will become a major part of your team's culture. Embracing this caring culture requires virtually no training, nor dollars spent. It requires compassion, caring, and the commitment to a simple follow through. Creating this one-on-one, potentially life-saving process will make a difference for your team. I challenge every person reading this book to implement this level of caring with the group or team you have influence with.

Dealing With suicide. Several times during my counseling and administrative career, the stormy weather associated with suicide impacted my team. At times, deciding whether to connect with another person or not becomes a life or death decision, and as the leader, the positive potential of connecting can be even stronger.

By actual count, I've dealt with the suicide attempts of over 30 people in my lifetime. I have spoken at many funerals and counseled with many surviving families and friends. I have led student and adult groups who sought to better understand the causes and the possible preventions of suicide. In virtually every suicide conversation I've been a part of, there were common threads. There was sadness and feelings of guilt in every group as friends and family members shared that they had known something was wrong, but had never reached out. Survivors share that they now know people love them and support them, but the reasons they gave for attempting suicide reflect loneliness and lack of connectedness: "Nobody cares about me," " Nobody has time for me," "I don't have any friends," "I had nowhere to turn for help," or, " I can't face this problem alone."

Suicides have a devastating impact. Unlike a fatal accident or health issue, suicide is especially difficult because family members and friends often feel guilt, as well as sadness. A specific step is to make professionally trained trauma therapists available to team members following the tragedy. Many professionals can be present on a volunteer basis, or as funded by an outside agency. During the work hours, team members can be encouraged to take advantage of available counseling services at any time they need support. In post-suicide groups, students and family may share times when the victim reached out, but their cry for help wasn't recognized. Because people in the group are experiencing both sadness and guilt, group sharing and support, facilitated by a trained professional, can often help the recovery process. Following steps outlined in this chapter's tables will help (see Table 9.1 and 9.2).

The reason for sharing suicide information in this book is that one of the primary causes of suicide, the lack of connectivity between people, can be addressed on every job site. Whether the business is education, manufacturing, medical, finance, or any other sector, connectivity can be a part of the culture in any setting. If a person seems down or withdrawn, team members at every level of the hierarchy can be challenged to approach the person, look them in the eye, and ask, "How are you doing?" If the person turns away or remains silent, walk with the person and ask, "Are you ok?" If the person says, "No" or will not respond, ask, "Will you come with me?" and escort them to an area where they can get support in a place that is safe and confidential.

Violent trauma. When faced with trauma caused by violence, such as a school shooting, the leader can employ many strategies outlined in this chapter (and in *The Ten Tools*) to manage the stress. It is even more important in these situations to have trauma counselors on hand for several weeks or months because everyone at the building, including the leader, will feel the impact of the stress caused by such severe violent acts. Though trauma counselors may be available on site for a limited time, team members might continue to suffer from Post Traumatic Stress Disorder (PTSD). The leader is not expected to treat mental illness; however, it will be the leader's job to recognize team members who might need more time or support to heal and be able to guide these team members toward the resources they need. Additionally, secondary trauma can be experienced by repeated exposure to media surrounding the event, and though the leader cannot control media consumption, you might encourage your team to refrain from engaging in social media immediately following the trauma.

Traumatic events in the world, such as the COVID pandemic in 2020-2021 or natural disasters (i.e. hurricanes tornadoes, floods, wind storms), also impact the team. Team members might have family members suffering, have lost jobs or income, or have suffered from mental health issues. During some of these situations, face-to-face communication may be impossible, and leaders have to rely on written and virtual communication with team members. It is even more difficult to connect with team members individually, and emotional weather systems can be unstable. In cases like this, leaders will need to rely on several of the steps presented Tables 9.1 and 9.2.

Any team that works together over a long period of time will eventually experience bad news. The trauma of a sudden death or other emotional event impacts every team member. In these situations, you will be a key player, in conjunction with crisis assistant teams, clergy, and trauma therapists, to support teammates through their grief cycle: shock, denial, anger, guilt, despair, depression, and acceptance. Timetables for recovery may vary widely among teammates and every team member has their own way of grieving. People will bounce back and forth between steps and will often experience multiple steps at the same time. It's both a test and an opportunity for a leader to lead the team with compassion, while processing your own sadness. The team will see you struggling with your own emotions, and this humanizing event will build trust, and team members will feel safer and closer to the leader.

As with the examples listed above, if traumatic occurrences have a serious impact on the emotional state of your team, you need to address the issue immediately. The negative situation should be treated as an event-inspired Doberman (see Chapter 5). Your quick actions should include clear communication about the issue and time for the team to share their feelings. Addressing emotional issues with the whole team allows for one consistent, accurate version to be delivered to every teammate. Though face-to-face communication may be tough on the leaders, the team will see and hear your courage and concern, and the team will appreciate and respect hearing the update directly from you. Your best efforts to control your own emotions and lead your team during these situations can earn credibility, and this type of interaction can be a strong team builder.

Stories About The Negative Impact of Stress on the Team

In the stories shared in Chapter 9, I focus on how a leader can lead in times of stress and work to control the emotional weather systems employees encounter on the job. "Leadership Lessons From Larry and Roscoe—Two Lab Rats" explores the types, causes, and impacts of stress. The rats teach us specific areas leaders can address to reduce the stress and improve the work environment. In Rick's story, "Changing Circumstances with a GED," readers can learn how stress can damage both mental and physical health, and learn how leaders can step up to provide support to team members as they escape from stressful situations.

Leadership Lessons on Stress from Roscoe and Larry—Two Lab Rats

This is not a story. It is science. I've included this account for two reasons. (1) The stressors that debilitate lab rats are the same stressors that debilitate humans. The simplicity of this stress/debilitate relationship is useful for creating solutions to address the stress side of the dichotomy. (2) Leaders can have a major impact on addressing such stressors as they build stronger trust bridges with their teams.

Over an 18-week semester, Roscoe and Larry were subjected to every type of reinforcement schedule and set of conditions imaginable. The experiments took place in a conditioning box that dispensed food pellets as a reward when the rats behaved as they should. The box had the ability to alter the environment in every conceivable way, including applying different levels of electrical shock into the floor grid. It turns out that Roscoe and Larry taught me some important fundamentals of psychology that didn't just apply to lab rats.

They learned faster and retained knowledge longer when their basic nutritional needs were met and their reinforcement schedules were consistent and predictable. They quickly got confused when reinforcement schedules were varied or inconsistent. Though leaders have little control over their team member's nutrition, they do have major control over how consistent and predictable they are when leading their teams (see "Traits of a 2 + 2 = 5 Team" in Table 8.1).

The rats' performance decreased when the rate or quality of the reinforcement decreased, which relates to the leader's commitment to strong communication and positive reinforcement (see "Small Hammer Strategies" in Chapter 2). Clear communication by the leader avoids confusion by teammates. Just as the rats responded to positive rewards, so too, do team members. Thus, developing positive relationships with team members in times of sunny weather is essential.

Finally, the rats panicked, became dysfunctional and reclusive, and suffered physically when their environment was changed. Such things as bright lights, loud noises, sprayed water, or electrical shock had a profound impact on their health and well-being. The breakdown happened even more quickly when the negative physical factors were combined, or if the rats were also sleep deprived. It often took a long period of time for Roscoe and Larry to return to their normal performance or behavior after being disrupted by physical stressors. Though the stressors in the rats' environment differed from stressors found in a human work environment, the responses were similar: panic, dysfunction, reclusiveness, and physical manifestations (see the Doberman analogy in Chapter 5).

Again, the crucial connection between Roscoe and Larry and you, and the members of your team, is that there will be times when you have control over the stressors in the work lives of your team (e.g. your behavior toward them), and there will be other times when you don't have control over the stressor (e.g. an external event). However, in either case, you do have control over your response to the stressor and your response to your teammates. By using the strategies suggested in tables 9.1 and 9.2, and throughout *The Ten Tools*, you can reduce stress for yourself and for your team, thus creating a healthier work environment for everyone.

Changing Circumstances with a GED

During my 18 years working in a large high school, I had observed a steady stream of adults and adolescents struggling and suffering while trying to navigate stressful experiences. By employing many of the tools described in this book, I was able to help manage stress in the workplace. I adopted a SIDWI (Chapter 1) approach to address emotional stress issues. I used flow time (Chapter 6) and careful hammer strategies (Chapter 2) to build healing bridges with these struggling individuals. I used Doberman strategies (Chapter 4) and I treated everyone right (Chapter 6). I tried to teach team members and students how not to major in the minors (Chapter 3). Each of these strategies worked with synergy to relieve teammates' and students' stress levels.

But when stress isn't addressed, the stress can take its toll in observable and unobservable ways. I took a special interest in the extraordinary stress that is present in some supervisor/employee relationships. A poor relationship between a student and their teacher, anticipated over 180 days is stressful for both parties. The same stress responses could be felt by a teacher who had a poor relationship with the department head. A major component, in both of these examples, is the inescapability factor. In Rick's story that follows, he also felt trapped by his supervisor.

I continued to learn more about the negative health impact of job stress when I began teaching an evening General Educational Development (GED) class at a nearby community college. Many of my students had dropped out of school due to personal issues and were now planning to use their GED diplomas to continue their education or to get better jobs. A few had already been successful in life and just wanted to be able to show their grandkids their diploma. I witnessed many that had high stress in their lives, but one student stands out.

In the first session of a new quarter, a man named Rick sat down in the front row of the class. He was a husky, good-looking 34 year-old guy, with a trucking company hat, a big smile, and a friendly personality. Rick stayed after class that first night. He wanted to tell me his story, and as he began, he started to sob. He told me about his great wife and two healthy kids, proudly showing me their pictures. Rick shared that he'd been working a job as a diesel mechanic for the past 12 years. During those years, Rick loved the job. It paid well, providing Rick's family with the means to build a nice, new home. He had built a strong trust bridge with his supervisor, who cared about him, and empowered him with training and encouragement. However, two months before I met Rick, the shop had been sold to a larger company and his boss and several of his closest co-workers had retired. Rick had never had a problem and his former supervisor had always praised his work. Rick's new supervisor was mean; he verbally bullied Rick daily. It was toxic. The stress had negative impacts on Rick's mental and physical health—even resulting in hair loss. He needed to get his GED so he could apply for a new job.

I had a knot in my stomach as I drove home to my own family that night. As the teacher for Rick's GED class, I knew that he was hinging his hope on starting a new career, on passing the GED test, on finding a new job. I knew he was relying on his own strength—and on me; I had to help him. I used many of the tools described in this book as I helped Rick toward his goal. I listened, I built trust bridges, I met one-on-one with Rick, and I showed him I cared. I remained calm and kept Rick focused on the job that needed to get done. I was patient with Rick as he learned new skills. And, Rick passed his GED. He found a new job with the opportunities created from his GED.

Conclusion

It is up to the leader to set an example when trauma and stress impacts the team. Tables 9.1 and 9.2 each include skills and strategies to help leaders during times of trauma. The leader's ability to support teammates and communities through crisis situations can strengthen the bridges necessary to start the healing process. When trust bridges are strong, the team is more likely to weather the storm together.

In the following table, think about the ways that you can lead in times of trauma. Ask yourself: What can I do to help team members? How can I remain calm during stormy weather? And how do I create more sunny days? Each of these questions should be considered as you create the action plan for this chapter.

Table 9.3
Action Plan: Addressing the Negative Impacts of Stress on the Team

What are two takeaways from this section?   1.   2.
What two strategies will you use to lead during times of stress and trauma?   1.   2.
What steps will you take now? (Action Steps for addressing the stress factors and outcomes with your team)

Note: This table provides another look at how leaders can identify and address the causes and impacts of stress on the team.

CHAPTER 10

TOOL #10: YOUR HEALTH AS A LEADER– OXYGEN MASKS AND STARFISH THROWERS

Chapter 10, the final chapter in this book, focuses on the most important and irreplaceable factor of them all— your physical and emotional health as a leader. Before you can use many of *The Ten Tools*, you will need to ensure that you are in good physical and emotional health. All of the questions that follow (and more) will be the focus of this final chapter.

- How does your body react when you're feeling lonely and vulnerable?

- How do you react emotionally? How does your personality change? Are you the same leader?

- How do you stay healthy?

- What are you doing to take care of yourself?

- How do you respond when you make mistakes?

- What happens to your team when you aren't healthy?

Leaders must care for themselves before they can care for their teams. In order to use SIDWI, choose the right hammer, or create a 2 + 2 = 5 team, the leader needs to be at 100%, so this final tool is one of the most essential tools in this book.

The chapter begins by examining the challenges leaders face when making decisions. When you need to make a final decision, it can leave you with feelings of loneliness and vulnerability. I will remind you of leaders throughout history that have felt lonely and vulnerable, which will provide insight and inspiration for dealing with your own lonely and vulnerable decisions. The next section in the chapter, "Who Says You are Always Right?", explores the need for leaders to be transparent with their teams, including admitting they were wrong. "Putting Your Own Oxygen Mask on First" and "A Tribute to Starfish Throwers" share strategies to sustain your health and build a team culture that will support your health into the future.

Making Decisions

Leaders often face difficult decisions in their work, and this section focuses on how the leader can practice self-care even when making those tough decisions. Life as a leader can be lonely and difficult, and leaders must make decisions that impact the livelihood of team members and the ultimate success of the team. Not everybody on the team is happy with the leader's decisions all the time, but the leader can feel satisfied that they did their best by following some of the tips included in the next sections. When leaders know they have done their best and considered all options when making decisions, even when the decision goes wrong, the leader can ensure their own emotional health.

Explaining Tough Decisions

When decisions become public, you will need to provide at least a general response. Keep your leadership filter activated, and practice some of the strategies shared in the public speaking tips (see Chapter 8).

You can ease tensions and help the team understand your decision when you acknowledge that the decision was a difficult one for you. Take the time to explain when you cannot share all of the details. Your team and other stakeholders need to understand and accept that you are not allowed to share certain information due to Federal Educational Rights and Privacy Act (FERPA), the Health Insurance Portability and Accountability Act (HIPAA), issues of attorney-client privilege, or the need to protect somebody's identity. Sharing information may not be important enough to risk the potential damage to an individual, a group of people, or an outcome.

There may be multiple opinions of how you should have handled the situation. It can be disarming to the critics when you admit that you may have missed a detail. But sharing that you considered all factors that were available at the time can increase confidence that you did your due diligence to make the decision you thought would be best for the team.

Making mistakes. I've been wrong plenty of times in my career. Many mistakes have been minor, and most have been correctable. Some mistakes are painfully obvious to anybody who is paying attention. Sometimes lack of knowledge or information might cause a mistake, but even with all the facts, leaders cannot anticipate the outcome of a decision until after it is implemented. In situations where I've made mistakes, even if I felt embarrassed or caught off guard, I found the best way to take care of my own mental and physical health was to remind myself that I had done everything I could to make the best decision at the time. This seemed to help me process my disappointment and prepare myself to move forward.

In my career, some of my most widely known mistakes involved hiring decisions, and some of my toughest hiring decisions occurred with high-profile coaching positions. In these situations, since coaches were particularly visible in the public eye, people often had strong emotional feelings about the team and its success. I was a professional baseball scout; I knew how to assess people's personality makeup (see Chapter 8); I used many scouting techniques when recruiting and hiring staff to my teams. However, much like baseball scouting, there were times when I didn't get it right. When I made unsuccessful hiring decisions, those who disagreed with my pick were the first to criticize. I responded to criticism with statements like, "I might have missed that one, but here is what I was thinking." A brief rationale showed the team the facts I considered at the time of the final decision and showed that I didn't make the decision without careful consideration.

Another public mistake I've made is when I've told the team something that turned out not to be true. This happens at times when facts change quickly. The leader may have told the team something was true, but facts changed, and it became false later. I remember an example when telling a group of math teachers that a certain textbook was going to be adopted for the math curriculum, only to find out later that the committee had changed its mind. Leaders often face this changing landscape during times of crisis, when decisions have to be made quickly without time for consideration. The leader may not be able to gather all the facts before a decision needs to be made, or the leader may relay a message from upper leadership, only for that same leadership to change their policy afterward.

Nobody is perfect, and most people appreciate and respect a person who admits they're wrong. When you learn that you've made a mistake, face the team head on. Avoiding the conversation only compounds the problem in the eyes of the team. An apology can earn the trust and credibility of your team and work toward building trust bridges: "If anyone was inconvenienced or hurt by my decision, I apologize." Being willing to admit you're wrong can make you seem approachable, and the more you practice admitting your mistakes, the easier it gets. When possible, I use appropriate, light-hearted humor, which allows the team and I to relax and build closer relationships.

Loneliness, Vulnerability and Self Care

History has taught us about famous leaders who have a lifetime of achievements. Mahatma Ghandi and Mother Teresa were strong, quiet people who gained fame by dedicating their lives to peace and caring for people. Both are remembered because they showed kindness and leadership in the face of oppression. Their nonviolent leadership approaches changed the lives of people they interacted with, and ultimately, the entire country of India. Other leaders gained fame due to "defining moments" and "defining decisions." Leaders, such as Winston Churchill, Martin Luther King, Jr., and John F. Kennedy, inspired people with their words. Their speeches and actions stirred their followers' hearts during challenging times.

Each of these legendary leaders experienced loneliness, especially during times of important decisions. This loneliness often stemmed from the fact that ultimately the decision was up to them. They couldn't rely on anybody else to make the decision, though they probably had advisors or a team behind them. Any leader today, may face that same loneliness and vulnerability when tough decisions have to be made. We ordinary leaders may not face world-changing decisions, but it is inevitable that at some time during our leadership journey, we will feel lonely and vulnerable when making a difficult decision for our team. That time may come when you have to make a major decision that is sure to disappoint or anger part of your team or stakeholders. You may feel lonely when only you have information, and you aren't able to share that information with anybody—even your spouse or closest confidant.

Not being able to talk through the decision might put a leader into a lonely and uncomfortable place. When a leader is accustomed to relying on their mentor's advice, not being able to go to that mentor and the necessity of making the decision on your own will be extremely hard. The two examples below, from my own career, were both event-inspired Dobermans (Chapter 5). The human dynamics leading up to, during, and after the conversations illustrate why the loneliness and vulnerability experienced in difficult decisions can be the toughest of self-care situations for a leader. Facing a Doberman situation head-on, as early as possible, can send a strong credibility message for any leader which creates trust, even with people who don't like the leader or don't agree with them.

A "mother bear" on a mission. I had heard about Heather Brown during interviews for my new position. Heather had a history of serious issues with the leadership and staff of my new district and her behavior had been a constant conversation point since my arrival. My board and staff advised that they had already learned the hard way—the best way to deal with Heather was through our attorney. My decision to meet with Heather one-on-one was not endorsed by my board or my staff. I was told: "We've tried that before" and "Buying Heather Brown a cup of coffee will be a total waste of your time and your money."

Heather sounded like she would be the toughest SIDWI challenge of my career, and it turned out she was. I was prepared to use every one of *The Ten Tools* to build a trust bridge with her. Our first meeting took place at her kitchen table with her husband present, which created a safe and secure environment for her. The emotional level was intense and hostile. As her husband sat silently, she spoke in loud, threatening tones about how she was going to sue the district again. I listened carefully and took 11 pages of single-spaced notes. I didn't take the lead at any time during this first meeting, and other than asking clarifying questions, slowing her down in a soft voice, "Whoa! Whoa! Still writing" and "rattling the tablet", I did nothing to interrupt her. I was determined to use only a finishing hammer, and it took all of my patience. The conversation was tense. After 90 minutes, we concluded the meeting and agreed to meet the following week to continue our conversation. I emailed Heather a thank-you note and put a written thank-you note in the mail.

I felt lonely and my chest tightened a little as I backed out of their driveway. For my own health, I knew I needed to give myself some physical and emotional separation from that meeting. I drove around listening to Frank Sinatra for thirty minutes before returning to my office. I had thought ahead and put "visiting elementary schools" on my calendar, and I spent the rest of my day visiting elementary buildings, soaking up the positive environments, and getting to know my new staff and students. Spending time at the elementary school was a perfect balm for my stressful day, and I left feeling much better than when I had arrived.

After a week of flow time, the next meeting was calmer. We still met at Heather's home, and Heather's husband was there again. Though he was still quiet, her husband's body language had relaxed. As her voice cracked, Heather thanked me for giving her a chance to share her side of the story. It was clear that the week of flow time between meetings had allowed her time to think. I had transferred some power to her, and now she wanted to hear what I thought; we had moved into the grey area. The small hammer approach, with SIDWI strategies had worked to begin building a trust bridge.

Heather and I continued to build a stronger trust bridge and I used, and re-used all of *The Ten Tools* as we co-existed in the grey area, developing solutions we could both agree on. Though neither of us ever got everything we wanted, our trust bridge was durable enough to develop some strong solutions for the benefit of her children, and that's all that mattered to her.

Though my emotional and physical health suffered during those early meetings with Heather, as our trust bridge grew, my sense of anxiety and stress dissipated, and I became a healthier person. I kept a tight leadership filter about my meetings with Heather, providing information only when it was needed for a team member to do their job. I avoided the extra stress load of having to re-process our meetings with any non-essential people. I continued to use stress reducing activities like taking a drive, exercising, visiting schools, keeping my confidant up to date and any other buffer activities that helped me to get better oxygen and stay healthy.

The issue with the coach. The following account is a SIDWI story about a meeting with a group of concerned parents about a coach at the high school. It was the young coach's first year at the varsity level. She had a team with below average talent who, in my estimation, had won all but one of the games they should have won. Of course, the parents believed that the team should have won all of their games and blamed the team's lack of success on the coach. I had heard rumblings in the community about the coach and the impending meeting. The group had invited any interested board members, but none chose to attend the meeting although three board members did inform me that it sounded like the coach needed to be fired.

Though personnel meetings such as this example, predictably carry an emotional and physical price tag for a leader, the short-term pain can be worth the long-term gain. With my background as a coach, my habit of attending virtually all of the activities in the district, and my experience as a leader, I felt prepared for the meeting.

Twelve community members were already seated around a table when I arrived at the meeting just before the scheduled 7:00 PM starting time. With my notepad in hand, I was able to stick with SIDWI strategies for the first three hours, listening, answering questions and taking notes. As I struggled to keep my body language under control, I couldn't help but think about the opinions shared by a majority of the school board members. The comments became more and more personal toward the coach: the wrong starters, wrong defense, wrong offense, wrong pep talk, wrong energy drink. Around 10:00 PM the leader of the group finally asked me what I was going to do. I told them I had watched 17 out of the 20 games they had played, in addition to approximately ten practices. I told them I had heard their concerns, but I believed that the young coach had earned another year to prove herself. This was a lonely decision, and I was vulnerable. The final hour of the meeting consisted of me being personally attacked by those angry parents. They threatened that they would have me fired and that they would bring their concerns to the next school board meeting, which they did. The board supported my decision and voted to give the young coach another year.

During these tough, lonely times, it is helpful to be able to share your thoughts with somebody you trust. Being able to share your feelings, along with communicating the key factors you considered while making your decision, will help you feel less stress throughout the process. For everyone but my confidant, I again used a tight leadership filter (Chapter 3) in dealing with this tough, lonely, and vulnerable situation. I don't share details of major stress events at work, or with my family. With teammates, I only share the level of information they need to know to process the outcome in their daily duties. I repeat— a key lesson in both of these stories is using your tight leadership filter to lessen your own stress by not having to process the anxiety and negative outcomes with others.

Putting Your Own Oxygen Mask on First

Physical, mental, emotional, and spiritual health are pillars of long-term personal happiness and inspired job performance for any leader. As you aspire to be an excellent leader for your team, nurture these same pillars for the team members at every opportunity. The trust bridges you build with your open, positive support of their personal well-being will be appreciated by your team. Give yourself permission to be part of the sunny weather that comes from having strong positive relationships at work. Value positive relationships and continue to look for ways to nurture them within your team. In addition to increasing your own strength and resilience, these strong trust bridges will help the team navigate the clouds and storms it will certainly face in the future.

On every flight, the flight attendants remind flyers that in the event of an in-flight emergency or loss of cabin pressure, they need to put on their own oxygen masks before helping anybody else. This flight analogy is clear— leaders need to take care of themselves in order to serve their teams.

Emotional Buffers

Leaders practice self-care by creating balance in their lives. One key to protecting emotional and physical health is to create emotional buffer zones or margins from the stresses of the job. These buffer/margin activities may be physical, such as the many types of exercise, or mental, such as reading, listening to music, meditating, or praying. Other oxygen sources can include activities such as vacations, trips, or even shorter escapes such as movies, concerts, sporting events, or other social opportunities. Each of these buffer activities can create a space for leaders to get air flowing through their oxygen masks.

Because these buffer activities can create joy, you should incorporate reminders into your work space. Items that bring pleasant thoughts for you may include looking at pictures of your family, a memento from a memorable event, or a picture of your favorite pet. Memorabilia such as concert or game tickets, pictures of a favorite travel spot, or beautiful nature pictures can also produce feelings of joy. A favorite soundtrack or inspirational quote can also help lessen the stress at work.

Try mentally labeling and recording your margin activities. For example, if you need to drive 20 minutes to a meeting or appointment, you may put in some music, listen to a book or podcast, or just enjoy the silence. At lunch time, if possible, leave the office: drive to a calming place, turn on your favorite music, and relax while you eat. During this buffer break, don't work. Don't check email or answer your phone. Force yourself to respect the break. Remind yourself that you're getting some margin time. Mentally recording your margin times helps you in two ways: (1) you can look for more margin times and (2) you will stay more aware of the margin times you were able to carve out in your day. Margin times relieve job stress and prepare you for the next tough appointment or challenge.

For me, the most important buffer time to carve out and protect is time with my family and other loved ones. As we shared with the concepts of the hourglass and golf ball (Chapter 3), putting your family times on your calendar and being firm about protecting those times ensures that you make time for self-care. A phone call or text saying that you have to work late, that you will miss or be late for dinner or an event, or cancelling time with your family simply doesn't work. There will always be more work on your list. But, there will not always be more family time and memories to make. To put it more bluntly, don't take the phone call if it's already after hours. Don't put in extra time if it means sacrificing your buffer activities. Go out to the parking lot, put your car in reverse and drive away. Doing this is the same as putting on your own oxygen mask first. Remember, you can only be as good at your job as your physical and emotional health allows you to be.

Finally, other people can help you find your buffer zone. Find a confidant outside of your profession, that you trust and can use as a sounding board. This person can focus on you as a person, rather than what's going on with your work. With this friend, you can blow off steam without it affecting a professional relationship. Remind each other of your hourglasses, and ask each other if you're investing your time and emotional energy on sand, gravel, or golf balls.

A tribute to starfish throwers. My challenge to readers of this book is to become a starfish thrower in every area of their lives (see Figure 10.1). As a leader, every team member, family member, or friend is a potential starfish. Create a team and family culture where every person is on the lookout for a chance to help someone else. Be the person who reaches down, picks up the starfish and helps them to safety. Being a starfish thrower may become the strongest buffer activity and oxygen source in your life.

Figure 10.1
The Starfish Thrower

Once upon a time there was a wise man who used to go to the ocean to do his writing. He had a habit of walking on the beach before he began his work. One day, as he was walking along the shore, he looked down the beach and saw a human figure moving like a dancer. He smiled to himself and thought of someone dancing to the day, and so, he walked faster to catch up. As he got closer, he noticed that the figure was that of a young man, and that what he was doing was not dancing at all.

The young man was reaching down to the shore, picking up small objects and throwing them into the ocean. He came closer still and called out, "Good morning! May I ask what it is that you are doing?"

The young man paused, looked up and replied, "Throwing starfish into the ocean."

"I must ask. Why are you throwing starfish into the ocean?" asked the somewhat startled wise man.

To this the young man replied, "The sun is up and the tide is going out. If I don't throw them in, they'll die."

Upon hearing this, the wise man commented, "But, young man, do you not realize that there are miles and miles of beach, and there are starfish all along every mile? You can't possibly make a difference!"

At this, the young man bent down, picked up yet another starfish and threw it into the ocean. As it met the water, he said, "It made a difference for that one."

Note: (Author Unknown, Available on Line and in Various Publications)

When Leaders Make Lonely Decisions to Achieve Big Outcomes

The first story shared in this chapter illustrates a time when I felt lonely and vulnerable during my time as a leader. The other two stories are further examples of the loneliness and vulnerability felt by two famous leaders at their decision times. Making tough decisions are a part of every leader's job, but being able to stand by your decisions and deal with the loneliness takes practice and courage.

The Ten Tools Heal an Entire District

In the following story, I share one of my most lonely and vulnerable times as a leader. When I was selected for the superintendent position in a new district, I discovered that I needed a plan that would unite the school board and the administrative team. Though both teams were successful in their respective jobs, they lacked strong trust bridges between each other as teams. I believed *The Ten Tools* would be my best chance to bring these two teams together for the good of the district.

I spent the months of July and August building trust bridges with board members and my new administrative team. I heard from board members, the administrative team, parents, and community leaders many reasons they were proud of their schools. But with a hint of nervous laughter, people in all three groups shared that there was room for improvement with the relationship between the school board and the administrative team. I felt strongly that improving their relationship was a challenge worth embracing, and I believed the stronger that their relationship became, the greater our potential would be as a district.

I viewed this as a major decision, and for the first time in my career, I decided to invite the school board members to join the administrative team for *The Ten Tools* orientation. Because of the existing issues of trust, I knew this would be an interesting—and challenging—workshop. When we met in the high school library for the orientation, every person from both teams was present. The body language was reserved as I circulated and greeted people. In my welcoming remarks, I didn't mention anything about the trust concerns I'd heard. I wanted them to spend the morning soaking in the human dynamics of *The Ten Tools*.

We began to talk about SIDWI, the 95% rule, sledgehammers, Dobermans, and majoring in the minors, and people began to share their own stories. They engaged in the content and really listened. There was sharing, laughter, and tears— of joy and of sadness. People were animated, and the volume was high. They were having fun together. One woman shared, "If I'd have known this stuff ten years ago, I'd still be married," and later confided to me that her comment was only partly in jest. After the meeting, people laughed and hugged as they headed out the door. The training had turned out to be an emotional experience for everybody, including me.

Afterward, I continued to hear positive feedback from both sides. Some enjoyed getting to see a new side of some of their teammates, and others expressed relief from sharing what had been on their minds for a long time. One of our key leaders told me, "I'm glad there was nothing on the agenda about an ice breaker or a team builder because our team always makes fun of those activities." Ironically, another veteran administrator said, "Boss, that was the best ice breaker and team builder I've ever seen. We really needed that."

Over six years, our team and board continued to experience success using *The Ten Tools*. Leaders who were facing tough personnel conversations came in and rehearsed SIDWI. As confidence and trust grew among the leaders, they began to rehearse, train, and mentor each other. The board felt empowered by their new trust with the administrative team. Clogged communication lines were opened up and a lot of healing took place.

Two Leaders at Lonely Crunch Times

Many years ago, my wife and I attended a national superintendent conference with 10,000 other attendees. One of the highlights was listening to the two inspirational and aspirational keynote speakers who shared their experiences of standing completely alone in a moment of decision. On back-to-back nights, world leaders, Mikhail Gorbachev and Ben Carson, shared intimate memories of feelings they had when they realized their decisions would determine the future's events. We all wanted to have the courage and clarity these men spoke of when we faced such lonely decisions.

The former General Secretary of the Communist Party of the Soviet Union, Mikhail Gorbachev grew up during the regime of Joseph Stalin. He worked closely with President Ronald Reagan to limit nuclear weapons and end the Cold War. Through a young interpreter, Gorbachev described pacing the floor of his apartment the night before standing in front of parliament and the people of Russia. After debates in parliament and demonstrations around Russia, it was up to Gorbachev to make the final decision about Russia's path and make the announcement. At the conference, he started his remarks in a robust voice, but as he described his feelings of loneliness and the high stakes of that night, his voice quieted. Gorbachev's message resonated with the leaders in the audience. The anxiety and feelings of loneliness and inadequacy before a big decision are the same in a small school district or on the world stage.

The following evening, Dr. Ben Carson spoke about the same feelings of loneliness he felt when a crucial outcome rested solely in his hands. Carson had become a world-renowned pioneer in neurosurgery, and that night he shared the story of his experience performing a successful operation on conjoined twins who shared parts of their brains. At the Johns Hopkins Hospital, Carson led a 70-person team to complete the 22-hour surgery. Carson described one point during the surgery when he decided to make an incision that could save both patients—or kill them. When both patients survived the surgery, Carson's decision made medical history.

During the remainder of the conference, school leaders shared their own examples of times when they had such lonely experiences making decisions. Common themes emerged: meeting with a team, gathering information on all sides of the issue, and making written notes were common preparation strategies.

Controlling body language, and using the microphone to allow a loud, clear voice also factored in, as leaders shared the challenge of keeping their heads up and maintaining eye contact, while trying to read their notes and manage their own emotions. Getting comfortable with responding to questions, saying "I don't know the answer to that question yet," was a common thread. Finally, predicting questions, and sticking to the facts were common responses.

Each of these leaders, and the thousands of leaders at the conference, shared experiences of loneliness and vulnerability at times when big decisions needed to be made. In this chapter, I shared strategies for overcoming loneliness and taking care of yourself. The tips I provided were similar to the themes that emerged long ago at that conference. Using strategies for preparation and self-care help you to feel calmer and more prepared for those tough decisions that are surely ahead on your leadership ladder.

Conclusion

In this chapter, readers explored the various pieces of self-care that leaders must practice. Making tough decisions is one of the hardest parts of leadership, and when leaders are faced with tough decisions, I share tips to ensure that they care for themselves in the midst of tough decisions. Being able to admit mistakes is difficult, but leaders can help their own emotional health when they can feel confident in their decisions, and this chapter shares ways for leaders to admit mistakes without losing credibility with the team. This includes feelings of loneliness and vulnerability that come when leaders must make decisions. Being able to take a walk, listen to music, call a confidante, or look at family pictures are all ways that leaders can take care of themselves on the job and make sure that their needs are not forgotten. Planning for buffer activities that create a space for leaders to destress and enjoy their relationships is essential.

Putting your own oxygen mask on first by staying healthy with life balance activities is crucial for long-term health and happiness in any leadership position. Creating and sustaining a caring culture where teammates look out for each other can improve the work environment and lead to a higher feeling of security and value for team members at every level. Sometimes it only takes one caring contact to make that difference. Develop the final tool, taking care of yourself, by completing Table 10.1.

Table 10
Action Plan: Your Health as a Leader—Oxygen Masks and Starfish

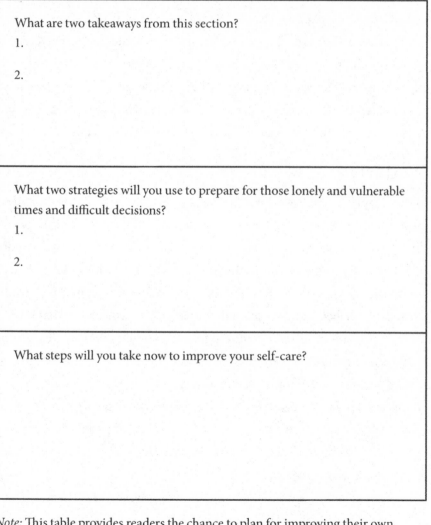

What are two takeaways from this section? 1. 2.
What two strategies will you use to prepare for those lonely and vulnerable times and difficult decisions? 1. 2.
What steps will you take now to improve your self-care?

Note: This table provides readers the chance to plan for improving their own health and to succeeding with difficult conversations with their team.

CONCLUSION

After reading this book, which tools do you see yourself actually trying?
In each chapter, you have completed an action plan that asked you to summarize key characteristics of each tool and come up with a next step. Use these action plans to practice the tools and each tool will become sharper. I suggest grouping the tools into the different areas of your life. Think of the tools you can use to strengthen bridges with your family and team, or with your friends. Practice will bring improvement and confidence as you take new risks and improve your skills and timing. Your family and your health are golf balls in your life, and you should be committed to investing the time necessary to making those bridges as strong as possible.

Each of *The Ten Tools* builds your leadership skills. Great leaders use the SIDWI steps constantly. To begin applying this tool to your leadership repertoire, you must mentally prepare to be a calm, patient, and engaged listener. This will help you start applying the glue for building trust bridges. Remember that you'll accomplish two things with your positive listening approach: (1) you will affirm to the other person that you value them and care about what they have to say, and (2) you will learn the details of where they are coming from and what is important to them. Finally, for SIDWI to work, you must be prepared to transfer power and to find the shared solution in the grey area. "Leave the sledgehammer in the pick-up" means you learn to select just the right hammer that will still get the job done. Don't major in the minors focuses on prioritizing. Use your hourglass and leadership filter to focus on what's most important. The 95% rule honors the majority of your team that is buying in, while firmly dealing with the 5% who aren't.

Remember the lessons of "You May Not be Able to Please Everyone, But You Can Treat Everyone Right." The power of high expectations, listening, flow time, and public relations is that when the public(s) and your team feel respected, great things can happen. "Don't Say Utilize" focused on adjusting your vocabulary and delivery to fit your audience. Position power focused on building 2 + 2 = 5 teams. Managing stress on the team requires leaders to deal with the weather systems on your team and to lead in times of trauma. Putting your own oxygen mask on first is a survival skill for your team, as well as for yourself, and creating a starfish throwing culture of caring on your team will empower a safe team environment.

Leaders can introduce the concepts presented in this book to their own teams—as professional development. Team members will enjoy using these new strategies with their coworkers and friends. They will also enjoy the sense of pride, excitement, and satisfaction that comes as they develop into 2 + 2 = 5 teams and stronger trust bridges are built.

Action Plan

Whether leading team members on the job, or with a family member at the kitchen table, connecting with another person in a positive way will always be a difference maker. Successfully handling emotions will also be a key factor in resolving tough human issues. As you become more skilled at using *The Ten Tools*, your ability to assist and support others will continue to grow. Combining your existing approaches with these tools will require courage and preparation when getting started. Mastering the sequencing of the tools and learning which tools seem easiest and most natural for you will become key.

In the following table, I provide some steps for you to start using the tools in your next meeting (see Table 11.1). When it's time to use one of the tools, review that chapter and jot down specific words that can help you successfully navigate the situation. If you're preparing for a tough, SIDWI conversation, re-read the scripts in the SIDWI chapter and plan to use exact words (mini-scripts) that will help you succeed with the meeting. Using the two lists from Table 11.1, begin matching up team or family situations with one or more of the tools you will begin trying out in real life. You can also start with somebody you already have a strong trust bridge with so you can use their feedback to improve your approach.

Table 11.1
Action Plan

Start by making two lists.

In the first list, divide all *Ten Tools* into one of three categories:
   1. I already feel very comfortable using this tool
   2. I was already aware of this tool, but I'm not proficient with it yet
   3. This tool is new for me, I need to practice it, and put the tool to work

The second list divides the type of situation into one of three categories:
   1. What situations at work or at home do I need to address now?
   2. Which tool(s) do I try first to address the above situations?
   3. What situation at work or at home may not be urgent, but may be important over the long haul? Which tools will I plan to use to create this longer-term outcome?

Note: This table provides tips for implementing *The Ten Tools for Success* into your work and personal life. Creating lists of specific situations will help you to begin integrating these tools in tangible ways.

Using *The Ten Tools* will bring you a sense of confidence and success to work toward stronger human bridges in every area of your life. Improving skills at building strong human bridges is a journey, and I hope you will join me in this process of ongoing improvement. It can enrich every area of your life.

Appendix A

Ten Tools for Success

1. SIDWI — Solve it-Don't Win It

    a. This tool requires the leader's attitude and choice

    b. Must solve the emotions, before you can solve the problem

    c. Listen, learn, transfer your power to find a solution in the grey area

    d. Build Trust Bridges to create emotional compromise - honor their feelings

2. Leave the Sledgehammer in the Pickup

    a. Preserve dignity, no bullies

    b. Take time to care

    c. Skilled leader uses the smallest hammer possible and still get the job done

3. Don't Major in the Minors

    a. Use the Hourglass Strategy

    b. Use the Leadership Filter

4. The 95% Rule - Don't Make Decisions Based on the 5% Who are Wrong

    a. Be patient and positive - 70% of what you are communicating is non-verbal

    b. Honor teammates that are doing things right

    c. Deal firmly and courageously with the 5% - send the right message

5. Don't Kick a Sleeping Doberman

    a. Don't look for trouble

    b. Know when to intervene and when to let your team solve it

    c. New leaders don't come in too hot

    d. Strictly honor the 95% Rule when dealing with Dobermans

6. You Can't Please Everyone, but You Can Treat Everyone Right

    a. Use the "Powers"

    b. Have high expectations

    c. Be a great listener— affirms the person and the leader learns something

    d. Use Flow Time - "You've given me a lot to chew on"

    e. Develop strong public relations

7. Don't Say "Utilize"

    a. Prepare in advance

    b. Adjust your language/vocabulary to each audience

    c. Use two-bit, rather than two-buck words

    d. Initials, acronyms and lingo are comprehension stoppers

8. Position Power - Personal Power Can be Stronger than Position Power

    a. Build a 2 + 2 = 5 team, trust, respect, synergy, focus on goals

    b. Promoted from within, new title— short term, relationships — long term

    c. Be patient, look for ways to solidify trust

    d. Appropriate Humor can be a positive team builder

9. Addressing the Negative Impacts of Stress in the Workplace

    a. Leaders control the weather for their team

    b. Leaders need joy too— build strong relationships with your team

    c. Encourage Soft Skills on the team, these skills can be the Elmer's glue

10. Your Health as a Leader—Oxygen Masks and Starfish

    a. Who Says You're Always Right?

    b. Put your own oxygen mask on first,

    c. Everybody needs their buffer activities

    d. Be a Starfish-throwing team, "How are you doing?"